THE
WISDOM
OF TANTRA

THE
WISDOM
OF TANTRA

An Introduction to Ananda Marga Philosophy

Dada Vedaprajinananda

InnerWorld Publications
San Germán, Puerto Rico
www.innerworldpublications.com

Published in the United States by InnerWorld Publications
P.O. Box 1613, San Germán, Puerto Rico, 00683

Library of Congress Control Number: 2016907337

ISBN: 9781881717515

Cover Design: Devashish Donald Acosta

Cover Ilustration: Aaron Staengl

SHORT SANSKRIT PRONUNCIATION GUIDE

- a is pronounced as the "u" in "us"
- á is pronounced as the "a" in "father"
- i is pronounced as in "bit"
- ii is pronounced as the "ee" in "beet"
- u is pronounced as in "put"
- ú is pronounced as the "oo" in "boot"
- e is pronounced as in "net"
- ae is pronounced as the "a" in "made"
- o is pronounced as in "top"
- ao is pronounced as the "o" in "owl"
- ṁ is pronounced as the "ng" in "sing"
- ṇ is pronounced as a nasal sound at the back of the throat
- ṭ, ḍ, and ṅ are pronounced with the tongue at the top of the mouth
- c is pronounced as the "ch" in "child"
- ph is pronounced as the "f" in "father"
- sh is pronounced as in "she"
- all other consonants followed by an "h" are aspirated (i.e. the original sound of the consonant followed by a "ha" sound)
- ś is pronounced between "sh" and "s"
- y is pronounced as "j" at the beginning of a word and "ia" in the middle or at the end of a word
- v is pronounced as "v" at the beginning of a word and "w" in the middle of a word
- jiṇá is pronounced "gyá", as in jiṇána (pronounced "gyána")

Contents

Preface

Forty-five years ago I first began reading the books of Shrii Shrii Ánandamúrti (1921-1990). Ánandamúrti was an Indian philosopher and spiritual teacher whose work spanned diverse fields of human endeavor, including spirituality, social science, science, linguistics, music and aesthetics.

In those books he laid out a spiritual philosophy that answered the big questions of life. How did the universe begin? What is the purpose of human existence? How does the mind work? What happens when we die? Is there a heaven or a hell? His books were not easy for me to fathom at first but after I familiarized myself with some new terms and concepts I was amazed by what I discovered.

The gist of Ánandamúrti's message to humanity is that we have all originated from one blissful, divine source and we are all on a return journey back to our point of origin. And, while we are on this journey of life, our main focus should be to do whatever we can to accelerate our spiritual development and at the same time to provide service to the entire universe.

When I turned my attention to Ánandamúrti's social writings (written under his civil name, Prabhat Ranjan Sarkar), I found an equally fascinating body of knowledge that provided a new look at persistent problems that have been dogging humanity since the dawn of time. How can we properly utilize and apportion the wealth of the world in a way that is fair to all? How can we bridge the differences that divide humanity? How can we end the exploitation of one human over another? Just as the spiritual books introduced a new philosophy of life, his social writings gave me a new framework in which to access economics, politics and related fields. I was exhilarated by this discovery and wanted to share it with everyone. That is why I became a missionary yoga monk for Ánanda Márga, the organization that Ánandamúrti founded. I went around the world teaching meditation and yoga and sharing my understanding of Ánandamúrti's spiritual and social vision. When I was teaching in France, in 1982, one of my students said, "Dada, we don't have books in French that can explain the philosophy properly." It was difficult to translate all of these books into French and other foreign languages in a short time, so I started to write a short book that gave an introduction to Ánandamúrti's spiritual and social writings. We published it in French in 1982 under the title *La Sagesse de Tantra*. In 1990 it was reprinted in the Philippines in English as *The Wisdom of Yoga*.

This little book then is a simplified introduction to the basic terminology and concepts that are found in all of Ánandamúrti's books. It was written to be a doorway that would hopefully make his books more accessible to general readers. Over the years many people told me that it helped them to understand this new school of philosophy. Unfortunately, *The Wisdom of Yoga* has been out of print for a number of years, and that is why we now present you with this edition.

When I began writing in 1982, Ánandamúrti had not yet finished laying down his philosophy, thus this new edition has an additional chapter on Microvita, particles that straddle the line between mind and matter. In addition, I have expanded on some of the original material and present a new chapter on cakras.

I hope that this book will help you to enter into the same glorious world of wonder that I first experienced in 1970, and that you will go on to study the original works upon which this volume is based.

Chapter 1

TANTRA: THE SCIENCE OF LIBERATION

Tantra is an ancient spiritual science first taught in India more than seven thousand years ago. *Tan* is a Sanskrit root which signifies "expansion," and *tra* signifies "liberation." Tantra is the practice which elevates human beings through a process in which their minds are expanded. Tantra can also be described as the practice that liberates human beings from crudity and dullness. Ultimately Tantra leads human beings from the imperfect to the perfect, from the crude to the subtle, from bondage to liberation.

The development of Tantra is intertwined with the development of civilization in ancient India.[1] During the time when Tantra emerged as an important spiritual practice, India was passing through a crucial historical period. In the Northwest, nomadic tribes from Central Asia, the Aryans, began to enter the country, which they named Bharata Varsha (the land which nourishes and expands human beings). Although the Aryans were a nomadic warrior culture, there were certain sages among them known as

1   This account of India's history and the origins of Tantra is based on the essay "Tantra and the Indo-Aryan Civilization," by Shrii Shrii Ánandamúrti, compiled in *Discourses on Tantra*, Ananda Marga Publications, 1990.

rishis who began to ask the basic questions about the origin and destiny of the universe.

These sages presented oral teachings, which were later compiled in books known as the Vedas. In these teachings they put forward the idea of a Supreme Consciousness and advanced beyond the previous concepts of a world in which many deities were thought to animate the forces of nature. They also developed a system of prayer and worship in order to enter into a relationship with this Supreme Consciousness, but their practices were mostly of an external, ritualistic nature.

In India the Aryans encountered and began to fight with the indigenous peoples—the Austrics, Mongolians, and Dravidians. They considered these races to be inferior, and in the epic tales of India, such as the *Ramayana*, these races are depicted as monkeys and demons.

However inferior these races were considered to be, the Aryans were very interested in the spiritual practices of the indigenous peoples of India. The spiritual approach of the non-Aryans was based on Tantra and it differed from the Vedic practices of the Aryans because it was fundamentally an introversive process rather than an external ritual. Many Aryans began to learn the Tantric system of spiritual development, and later Vedic books were influenced by Tantra.

During this era of warfare between the Aryans and non-Aryans, a great personality was born. His name was Sadashiva, which means "he who is always absorbed in consciousness and one whose only vow of existence is to promote the all-around welfare of living beings." Sadashiva, also known as Shiva, was a great spiritual preceptor or guru. Although Tantra was practiced before his birth, it was he who for the first time gave humanity a systematic presentation of spirituality.

Not only was he a great spiritual teacher, but he was also the founder of the Indian system of music and dance, which is why he is sometimes known as Nataraja (the Lord of the Dance). He invented Tándava, the jumping dance depicted in the statues of Nataraja, and his wife Parvati invented Lalita Marmika, a graceful dance practiced in devotional congregations. According to Ánandamúrti, the word *tala*, which refers to the basic rhythms of Indian music, is a combination of "ta" from Tandava and "la" from Lalita Marmika. Shiva was a skilled singer and was called "Nádatanu. " Ánandamúrti also credits Shiva with the invention of the seven-note scale (*surasaptaka*) of Indian music.

Shiva was also a founder of Indian medicine. Prior to Shiva there was a form of Ayurveda practiced in India, but Shiva systematized medical practice into a body known as Vaedyak Shastra. The Vedas placed restrictions on touching the bodies of so-called lower caste people, which hampered the use of dissection and the development of surgery. Shiva's Tantra-oriented system had no such limitations and surgery was practiced even in this ancient era. According to popular lore, Shiva knew many remedies and was thought to be immortal, hence he was given the name "Mrtyuinjaya" (Conqueror of Death). Today in Indian there is a popular saying: "Even Shiva has no cure for this disease."

In the social sphere, too, Shiva had an important role to play. He introduced a system of marriage in which both partners accepted mutual responsibility for the success of the marriage, regardless of caste or community. Shiva himself was of mixed parentage, and by marrying wives from the Aryan, Mongolian and Dravidian communities he helped to unite the warring factions of India and gave them a more universal social outlook. Because of these social innovations Ánandamúrti called Shiva "the father of Indian civilization." [2]

According to Ánandamúrti, Shiva's greatest contribution to the birth of civilization was to introduce the concept of dharma. Dharma is a Sanskrit word which signifies the innate characteristic of something. What is the innate characteristic and specialty of humans? Shiva explained that a human being wants more than the pleasure provided by sensory gratification. He said that the human being is different from plants and animals because what he or she is striving for is absolute peace. This is the goal of human

2 See Ánandamúrti's book *Namah Shivayah Shantaya* for an appraisal of the life of Shiva and his teachings. Ánandamúrti's Shiva is not the mythical god of the Hindu pantheon but an actual historical being.

life, and Shiva's spiritual teachings were aimed at enabling any human being to attain this goal.

Like most ancient teachings, Shiva's ideas were first taught in oral form, and only later were they transcribed into books. Shiva's wife Parvati used to ask him various questions regarding the spiritual science. Shiva replied to these questions, and the compilation of these questions and answers are known as the Tantra Shastras (Tantric scriptures).

Some of these ancient books have been lost and others are indecipherable due to their having been written in a code language designed to keep the secrets of Tantra away from the uninitiated; thus the ideas of Tantra have never been clearly explained.

Guru and Disciple

In his commentaries on the Tantra Shastra[3] and in his book about the life and teachings of Shiva, Ánandamúrti has presented some of the basic ideas found in the ancient teachings. One of the most important elements in Tantra is the relationship of guru and disciple. Guru means "one who can dispel darkness" and Shiva explained that for spiritual success there must be a good teacher and a good disciple.

Shiva described three major categories of guru. The first type is a teacher who gives a little bit of knowledge but does not follow up the lessons. That is, he or she may leave and the disciple is then left alone without guidance. The second or middle level is one who teaches and then guides the disciple for a little while but not for the complete period needed by the disciple to reach the final goal. The best type of teacher according to Tantra is one who gives a teaching and then makes continued efforts to see that the disciple follows the instructions and finally reaches the ultimate state of human perfection.

---

3   See the essay "Tantra and Sadhana" in *Discourses on Tantra, Volume 2* for a full description of some of the fundamental concepts found in the Tantra Shastras.

The qualities of this highest guru are further enumerated in the Tantric scriptures. The guru is one who is tranquil, can control his or her mind and is humble and modestly dressed. He or she earns his or her living in a proper way and is a family person. He or she is well versed in metaphysical philosophy and established in the art of meditation. The guru is someone who knows the theory and practice of imparting the teaching of meditation, and loves and guides the disciples. Such a guru is called *Mahákaola*.

But even if there is a great teacher, there must also be someone who can absorb the lessons. The Tantric scriptures describe three different categories of disciples. The first type is compared to a glass which is placed in the water with the mouth facing downward. While it is in the water it appears to be full but if it is lifted out of the water it becomes empty. This is like a student who practices well in the presence of the teacher, but after the teacher leaves, the student discontinues the practice and cannot apply the teachings to his or her everyday life.

The second type of disciple is like someone who climbs up a tree to pick fruit and hastily places them in a fold in his clothing but does not take care to see that the fruits are safely secured. When he or she descends from the tree many pieces fall on the ground. Disciples in this category practice the spiritual lessons in the presence of the teacher but after a while their ardor diminishes and they eventually lose interest in following a spiritual way of life.

The third kind of disciple is the best of all and is symbolized by a glass that is immersed in the water in an upright position. While in the water it is completely full and when it is taken out of the water it remains full. This kind of student practices in the presence of the master and continues the practice even if he or she is physically separated from the teacher.

The relationship of guru and disciple is very important and is a key feature of Tantra. The path of spirituality has been described as being as thin as a razor's edge. At any moment it is possible to deviate from the path and then it is very difficult to reach liberation. The guru is always there to love and guide the disciple at all stages of the practice.

Shiva was a Mahákaola, but after his death there was a lack of teachers of the same stature and Tantra fell into decline. Some of the teachings were lost and others were distorted. Today Tantra is shrouded in mystery and there are many misconceptions about it. To understand the source of these misconceptions it is important to examine the five M's. These are spiritual practices beginning with the letter M. Shiva gave his lessons with an eye to the capacity of each student. He saw that certain people were at a level in which they were dominated by animal passions and others were at a higher stage of development. He gave different practices depending on the qualities of the disciple.

The Five M's

The first M is known as *madya*. It has two meanings. One meaning of *madya* is "wine." For those people who were dominated by physical instincts Shiva instructed them to continue drinking wine, but he showed them how to control the habit and then finally leave it. For those at a higher level of development *madya* has another meaning; it refers not to wine but to divine nectar. According to yoga, each month the pineal gland secretes a fluid known as *amrta*. A yogi who has purified his or her mind and practices fasting can taste the fluid and experience the profound effect of this *amrta* on his or her whole being. This experience has been described as a state of bliss. Thus, there is both a crude or material interpretation of *madya* and a subtle or spiritual understanding of the term.

Another of the five M's is *mámsa*. One meaning of *mámsa* is meat. For those who ate much meat, Shiva told them to continue to eat it, but with spiritual ideation, and finally to control the urge and quit the habit. For the subtle practitioner of Tantra, *mámsa* refers to the tongue and the spiritual practice of controlling one's speech. In addition, the term *mámsa* is also used to describe the subtle state of devotional love for the Supreme Consciousness.

Matsya, the third of the M's, refers to fish. For the physically-minded practitioner Shiva applied the same instruction regarding fish as he did with wine and meat. In spiritual or subtle Tantra fish refers to two subtle nerves that run up the spinal column, starting at the base of the spine and crisscrossing each other, ending in the two nostrils. These nerves are known as the *ida* and *pingala*. By the science of breath control, práńáyáma, the currents of the nerves are controlled and the mind becomes calm for meditation. This is the *matsya* of the spiritual practitioner.

Another of the M's is *mudrá*. *Mudra*, in its material sense, has been associated with the consumption of certain food, but in its spiritual sense it has nothing to do with food. *Mudra* means to maintain contact with those who help us to make spiritual progress and to avoid the company of those who might harm our development. Keeping good company is also known as *satsauṇga*, and it is a crucial component in spiritual practice.[4]

The last of the M's, *maethuna*, is the one that has caused the most confusion regarding Tantra. *Maethuna* means "union." In its crude sense it means sexual union. For those who were dominated by the sexual instinct, Shiva said that the sex act must be done with spiritual ideation and that gradually this instinct must be controlled. For the more advanced practitioners, those who were practicing subtle or spiritual Tantra, Shiva taught another practice of *maethuna*. In this case union refers to the union of individual consciousness with Supreme Consciousness. According to Tantra, the spiritual energy of the human being, lying dormant at the base of the spine, is raised until it reaches the highest energy center (near the pineal gland), causing the spiritual aspirant to experience union with the Supreme.

The Ánanda Márga yoga taught by Ánandamúrti is based on the subtle spiritual interpretation of the five M's. And indeed, most of what is taught as yoga around the world today is based on the subtle five M's of Tantra.

---

4 Besides this definition of mudra in the context of the five m's, the term is also used for two other important practices of yoga. Mudra also denotes a type of exercise, similar to yoga postures, used to improve psycho-physical functioning of the body. Mudras also refer to gestures used in dance and music.

Mantra and Meditation

One of the distinctive aspects of subtle Tantra is its method of meditation. The concept of mantra is of key importance in the Tantric idea of meditation. In Sanskrit *man* means "mind" and *tra* means "that which liberates," and thus mantra is a particular vibration that liberates the mind.

The ancient yogis experimented with sound vibration and began to utilize special sounds that they found useful in the process of mental expansion. They found that there are seven principle psycho-spiritual energy centers in the human body. They further learned that there are fifty sounds that emanate from those centers. These sounds constitute the Sanskrit alphabet, and certain combinations of the sounds were used in ancient processes of concentration and meditation. During Tantric meditation the meditator concentrates on the mantra and tries to keep only one sound vibration (and its associated idea) in his or her mind. Constant repetition of the mantra leads a practitioner to higher states of consciousness.

Not just any sound can be chosen at random for use in meditation; rather there are certain qualities that the mantra must possess in order for it to be effective. First of all, the mantra must be pulsative; that is, it must have two syllables that are repeated in synchronization with the inhalation and exhalation. In addition, the mantra must have an idea associated with it. The general idea of the mantras used in meditation is "I am one with the Supreme Consciousness." The mantra thus helps the individual to associate his or her own individual consciousness with the totality of consciousness in the universe.

The final characteristic of the mantra is that it must create a certain vibration that acts as a link between the individual vibration of the meditator and the vibration of the Supreme Consciousness. As people are not all alike, the mantras used in meditation are also not all alike. The meditation teacher chooses a mantra that matches the particular vibration of the individual and can link this individual vibration with the universal rhythm of the Supreme Consciousness.

Diikśá: Spiritual Initiation

The Tantric process of imparting a mantra is called *diikśá.* There is no English equivalent of this word. The word "initiation" is often used to describe this event but it does not really tell what happens when a student learns a mantra from a teacher. The Sanskrit word *diikśá* can be broken down into two parts. *Dii* comes from the term *diipaŋjinánam,* which means "light of knowledge." *Ksha (kśa)* comes from the term *pápakśayam,* which means "waning or exhaustion of past karma *(saḿskáras).*"

Ánandamúrti explains *diipajiṇánam* as follows: "Suppose you have to travel to a certain place in the dark along a path strewn with sharp stones and boulders. If you attempt to take even one step forward you might fall down and injure yourself. So, you should take a lamp with you. This is called *diipajiṇánam.*[5]

The lamp he is referring to is the process that helps an aspirant move through darkness and practice properly. At the time of spiritual initiation a technique is given to the student, helping him or her to concentrate properly.

Ksha or *kśa* comes from the Sanskrit word *papakśayam,* which means exhaustion of saḿskáras (or past karma). The process of practicing meditation makes it possible for an aspirant to move past the burden of past actions. Through meditation the past actions are "satisfied on the psychic plane, thus freeing that person from the bondages" of past actions (from the essay "Diiksha and Initiation"). Sometimes a new meditator will feel either extremely happy or extremely sad right after the spiritual initiation. This is a sign that *papakśayam,* or the destruction of past saḿskáras is taking place.

Ánandamúrti further explains that the process of moving beyond the fetters of the past requires two other factors. When someone repeats a properly prescribed mantra, a vibration is created that strikes or vibrates the sleeping spiritual force (kundalini) and that force starts an upward movement. This upward movement is a part and parcel of spiritual awakening. The action of the mantra striking or arousing the kundalini is known as *mantrághata.* The

---

5 "Tantra and Sadhana," compiled in *Discourses on Tantra, Volume 2.*

upward movement of the kundalini is called *mantra caetanya*, and Ánandamúrti says, "with the help of ... *mantrághāta* and *mantra caetanya*, a spiritual aspirant is freed from all the mundane bondages, bondages both on the physical and on the psychic plane." In mantra meditation it is important for a person to understand the meaning of the mantra and that is why Ánandamúrti declares that *mantra caetanya* literally means "to imbibe the proper spirit of a mantra." If a mantra is repeated with the understanding of the inner spirit, *mantra caetanya* will be an easier task. To repeat the mantra without understanding its spirit is a waste of time.

The Spirit of Tantra

Tantra is more than just a collection of meditation or yoga techniques. There is a particular worldview associated with it. According to Tantra, struggle is the essence of life. The effort to struggle against all obstacles and move from the imperfect to the perfect is the true spirit of Tantra.

Ánandamúrti also notes that "every sádhaná (spiritual practice) that aims at the attainment of the Supreme, irrespective of its religious affiliation, is definitely Tantra, for Tantra is not a religion; Tantra is simply the science of sádhaná (spiritual practice)." He also points out that "wherever there is any spiritual practice it should be taken for granted that it stands on" Tantric practice.[6]

According to Tantra, in this movement from imperfection to perfection, there are three basic stages an individual passes through. In the first stage, the person is dominated by animal instincts, but in the next stage he or she gains control over these instincts and reaches the state of true human development. Finally, by constant struggle and effort, a state is reached where the human being becomes godlike. Tantra thus has an optimistic worldview. It shows how each individual is moving in a cosmic cycle from a state of less-developed consciousness to the most highly developed status.

---

6   "Tantra and Its Effect on Society," compiled in *Discourses on Tantra, Volume 2.*

Chapter 2

WHAT IS DHARMA?

As mentioned previously, the explanation of dharma was one of the main contributions that Shiva made to human civilization. Dharma is a term that is frequently mentioned in texts on Eastern philosophy and religion, but it is often misunderstood. It is usually translated simply as religion or social duty.

Shiva's concept of dharma, however, was a bit wider. He, and Ánandamúrti after him, explained that dharma refers to the innate characteristic of any being or thing. For example, fire is identified by its burning capacity. Without this burning capacity we would not be able to label it fire. The dharma of fire is to burn things. Similarly, plants and animals have certain defining characteristics that define them as plants or animals. These essential characteristics are their dharma.

Thus, eating, sleeping, fear and procreation are the basic qualities or dharma of animals. What about human beings; what is our dharma? This is the kind of knotty question which schoolteachers like to ask their students from time to time. They might ask, what is it that sets humans apart from animals?

Sharp students might reply that we humans have linguistic ability. And a sharp teacher will point out that whales and other creatures have intricate communication abilities as well. Other students might mention the human capacity to build magnificent structures, but once again the astute teacher will point out that some animals, including the lowly ants, are also good builders. Tool using and tool making were once thought to be the exclusive domain of homo sapiens but we now know that other primates also use tools and even make them, as well.

So what really sets us apart? Are we just naked apes with advanced diplomas and degrees from prestigious universities? The yogis say that although we share the basic dharma of eating, sleeping, fear and procreation with animals, we also have a special dharma that sets us apart from animals. This special nature is that human beings are not content with finite physical pleasures; they can only be truly satisfied when they merge their individual consciousness with the Supreme Consciousness. This unique quality is termed *mánava* (human) dharma and it is also called *bhágavata* (divine) dharma.

There are four stages to the practice of human dharma. The first step is expansion of mind (*vistara*). We human beings are not content to remain in a mental cage. We want to expand our horizons. This natural urge is one reason why totalitarian systems that attempt to limit freedom of thought are doomed to failure.

In the context of spirituality and meditation, expansion of mind has a great role to play.

Instead of thinking "I am an entity confined in a bag of skin and bones," when I meditate I imagine that my consciousness, my true being, is growing wider and wider until it embraces the entire cosmos. Expansion of mind is letting your mind explore and find out who you really are. This process of mental expansion is the first part of spiritual practice, but it is also a tendency that is innate in all humans, and it is one of the reasons why humanity has progressed so much in the last fifteen thousand years.

The second aspect of human dharma is called *rasa* in Sanskrit and flow in English. It means merging our minds in the cosmic rhythm. Normally we act using our ego and often we are not able to accomplish what we want because our individual desire conflicts with the greater flow of the universe. There is an old saying that goes, "Man proposes and God disposes." However, as a person goes further into the practice of human dharma, he or she begins to understand and feel that there is a cosmic rhythm, and slowly but surely he or she begins to flow with the cosmic rhythm. Life becomes easier, just as it is easier to paddle a boat in the direction of the flowing water than to try to paddle against the current. When a person flows with the cosmic rhythm, he or she feels that the real "doer" of life's actions is not the individual ego but the Cosmic Consciousness. Getting into this flow is joyful and it is the second stage of human dharma.

As a person expands his or her mind and begins to experience the flow of the entire universe, there arises the desire to serve other living beings. Selfless service is called *seva* in Sanskrit and is the third component of human dharma.

What the yogis mean by service is different than the current usage of this word in television advertisements. Often some business will proudly claim that "we have been serving the public since 1800"; however, they have been doing business and not service. In business there is a transactional exchange. Someone gives money and another person gives something in exchange (either a physical product or some work). It is a mutual process. However, service is unilateral. Someone gives something but does not ask for anything in return.

As a person goes deeper into spirituality, service-mindedness becomes part of his or her nature. That person sees other beings as an expression of the Divine and offers service without seeking financial gain or social recognition. The sacrificing nature and service-mindedness of people whom we refer to as saints is an example of how this quality becomes prominent as one advances on the path of human dharma. But you don't have to be proclaimed a saint to practice *seva*. Each of us, as we grow and express our higher nature, can and will serve others because it is our basic nature. It is what we came here to do.

The result of this process of expansion of mind, flowing with the cosmic rhythm and service, is unification with the Supreme

Consciousness. The yogis call this *Brahma Tadsthiti*. or merger in the Supreme Consciousness. This is the final point of human existence. This is what humans are striving for, knowingly or unknowingly.

Longing for the Great, longing to become one with the Supreme Consciousness, is what sets humans apart from other living beings. Biologically we are mammals. We share some basic qualities with animals, but we also have the possibility to walk on the path of human dharma and expand our minds, to flow with the cosmic rhythm, serve others, and finally merge with the ultimate source of all being.

It is because of this thirst for limitlessness, for a happiness that does not end, that human beings are usually unsatisfied with their lot in life. Even a very rich person will tell you that he or she is worried that the stock market may go down and all his or her wealth will be lost. According to the yogis, true fulfillment comes when we walk on the path of human dharma.

Chapter 3

AŚTÁUṆGA YOGA: EIGHT STEPS TO PERFECTION

The goal of Tantra is complete happiness and the method for attaining it lies in the full development of mind and body. Although this perfection of mind and body can be achieved slowly through natural means there is also a well-defined method for more rapid self-development. There are eight parts of this practice and since its goal is union (yoga) with the Cosmic Consciousness, it is also known as *Aśtáuṇga* yoga (often transliterated as Ashtanga) or eight-limbed yoga.

The first two steps are *yama* and *niyama*, which are moral guidelines for human development. The idea is that by controlling our behavior we can achieve a higher state of being. We are not simply following a rule for the sake of following a rule. Rather the object is to attain perfection of the mind. When this state is attained then there will be no question of "rules" because the desire to do something that is detrimental to our own welfare or that of another person will no longer be present in the mind. This is a state of perfect equilibrium.

Yama means "that which controls," and the practice of yama means to control actions related to the external world. In his book

A Guide to Human Conduct, Shrii Shrii Ánandamúrti has clearly explained the different aspects of yama and niyama, giving an interpretation that is clear and also practical for people in the present era. Here we will briefly review the five parts of yama and the five parts of niyama. For a fuller explanation one should read *A Guide to Human Conduct.*

The first principle of yama is *ahiṁsá.* Ahiṁsá means not to harm others by thought, word or deed. To the best of our capacity we should never inflict injury on another living being. This principle is sometimes interpreted to mean complete nonviolence, but if carried to an extreme it becomes very impractical. For example, each time we breathe there are microbes that we inhale and kill! In addition, whenever we eat anything, even vegetables, some form of life is injured. To solve this dilemma Ánandamúrti suggests that in selecting our diet we should choose food where consciousness is less developed rather than killing highly developed creatures.

Another problem is the question of self-defense. Here Ánandamúrti says that it is justifiable to defend oneself against an aggressor or against an antisocial person. Even if you use force, your intention is to save and protect life, not to cause pain or block the mental, physical or spiritual progress of that person.

The second principle of yama is called *satya.* The definition of satya is "action of mind and the use of speech in the spirit of welfare." It means to tell the truth and act in a straightforward and honest way that will promote the welfare of all. In cases where telling the exact truth will harm others, then satya means to say what is best for the welfare of others rather than to tell the exact facts. Adherence to satya brings about tremendous strength of mind and is extremely important for spiritual success as well as worldly success.

The third principle is *asteya.* Asteya means not to take possession of things that belong to others, that is, one should not commit theft. In addition, stealing should not be done mentally. Those who want to steal but who refrain from doing so out of fear of being caught are "mentally" stealing. Asteya means to cease both mental and physical stealing.

In addition to direct theft, another kind of stealing is depriving others of their due. If someone sneaks into a theater without paying, he or she has not taken anything directly but has deprived the theater owner of what was due to him or her. Like direct theft, this kind of indirect theft can be done mentally, too, and the spiritual practitioner should avoid doing it.

The fourth principle is *brahmacarya*, which means to remain attached to Brahma (the Cosmic Consciousness). This is practiced by treating all beings and things as an expression of the Cosmic Consciousness. The mind takes the shape of the object of our thought. If we are thinking in a materialistic manner, seeing things only as material objects, then our minds will gradually become dull. If we can perform all actions remembering that everything in this world is actually the Cosmic Consciousness in a transformed state, then our minds will move toward a state of oneness with the Cosmic Consciousness. In some books brahmacarya has been described as sexual abstinence. This definition was put forward in the middle ages by priests who wanted to attain supremacy over family people.

The fifth part of yama is *aparigraha*, which means not to hoard wealth that is superfluous to our actual needs. It means to live a simple life with only as much physical wealth as is actually necessary. This amount is variable according to time, place, and person. Aparigraha is an important principle in both individual and collective life, because if one person or one nation hoards wealth, it may result in starvation and misery for other people. It is an important part of spiritual practice, because if one is always preoccupied with physical objects, then he or she cannot think about the Cosmic Consciousness. As we shall see when looking at the principles of self-regulation, learning how to control one's accumulation of wealth also has important psychic effects for any individual.

The second major part of Aśtáuṇga Yoga is called *niyama*. Niyama means "self-regulation" or practices that help us to maintain inner harmony. Without self-regulation, it is impossible to attain higher states of consciousness.

The first principle of niyama is *shaoca*. Shaoca means "purity of mind and body." It includes cleanliness of one's external world, such as one's body, clothing and environment, as well as the internal world of the mind. External cleanliness can be achieved by regular cleaning of the body and the environment, while internal purity of mind can be attained by auto-suggestion. That is, one must substitute a good thought in place of a destructive thought. For example, if one feels greedy, one should think about and then perform a generous action.

Purity of mind also depends on how we handle the stimuli we get from our external environment. In this regard, Buddha told his monks to withdraw from seeing, hearing, tasting or smelling anything that would degrade them, and his instructions for all-around self-restraint are still valid today.

The second part of niyama is *santośa* . It means to maintain a state of mental ease. When the mind hungers for something it is in a state of uneasiness. Upon satisfying that desire, the moment of relief and ease that the mind experiences is called *tośa* in Sanskrit. Those people who are easily satisfied and can maintain a state of contentment are following santośa.

The achievement of santośa is linked with aparighraha, because people who accumulate excessive wealth never find satisfaction or contentment. It is ironic that the wealthy people who we would expect to be happy and content are often more psychically troubled than so-called poor people.

Following santośa means to do one's labor and then be satisfied with the results of that labor and not to hanker for more and more physical goods. However, it does not mean that you should allow others to exploit you. What it does mean is that after fighting for and obtaining your legitimate rights, you should not go on desiring more and more physical wealth.

Regarding santośa or contentment, Ánandamúrti has observed that there are two examples of contentment in the animal kingdom, one that is good and one that is bad. The good example is the dog, an animal that is easily satisfied with some food and a pat on its head. A bad example is the honey bee, a creature that toils endlessly, even though its hives are filled with honey, and consequently lives a very short life. The third principle of niyama is *tapah*. It means to undergo hardship on the path of personal and collective development. An act that is done in the spirit of service, helping others without expecting anything in return, is considered tapah. Service should be rendered to people who really need help. If you undergo suffering to feed a rich person, it is not a very useful service. In the past some spiritual aspirants practiced self-inflicted hardships and austerities (like walking on fire or even beating themselves) but such austerities do not provide benefits to the aspirant, to the society or to Cosmic Consciousness, so they have no importance in spiritual advancement.

Tapah aids the spiritual aspirant because it helps him or her to overcome the ego. Normally someone who tries to meditate is distracted by thoughts of the various problems that he or she is facing. Oftentimes, when someone engages fully in selfless service he or she will simply forget petty personal problems and be able to sit down for meditation and finally enjoy the peace of higher consciousness.

The fourth principle is *svádhyáya*. It means having a clear understanding of a spiritual subject. One should read and assimilate the meaning of great books and scriptures written by spiritually advanced people. Mere reading without understanding is not svádhyáya. The importance of svádhyáya is that it gives one contact with great personalities and inspires one to continue on the path of self-realization.

The fifth part of niyama is *Iishvara praṅidhána*, which means to make the Cosmic Consciousness the goal of your life. This is done through a process of meditation in which the meditator thinks only of one thought, the Cosmic Consciousness. As previously explained, in Tantric meditation the meditator repeats a mantra that reminds him or her of his or her relationship with the Cosmic Consciousness. Part of this meditation process also includes steps where the mind is detached from other objects and is focused on the Cosmic Consciousness. In the process of Iishvara praṅidhána the goal is to make the mind one-pointed and to direct it to the Cosmic Consciousness.

The third limb of eight-limbed yoga is ásana. An ásana is a posture that is comfortably held. It is the most well-known part of yoga, but it is often misunderstood as well. Ásanas are not normal exercises such as calisthenics or gymnastics. Ásanas are special exercises that have specific effects on the endocrine glands, joints, muscles, ligaments and nerves.

The earliest ásanas were developed in the antiquity of human civilization, perhaps more than seven thousand years ago. No one knows who invented these ásanas. According to Indian folklore, some ásanas were developed by sages based on their observation of wild animals. The yogis watched the movements of animals and then imitated them, hoping to acquire some of the positive qualities of those particular animals.

Whether that's true or not, there are several ásanas named after animals that do help humans to develop worthwhile traits. For example, the peacock is a bird with a powerful digestive system, capable of digesting even a poisonous snake. When a yogi assumes the peacock ásana and balances his or her extended body on his or her elbows (thus resembling the shape of a peacock), the pressure that is exerted on the organs in the abdominal area has an extremely beneficial effect on the yogi's digestive system.

Similarly, Ánandamúrti says: "The tortoise can easily retract its extremities. If human beings can also sit in that way for some time, they can withdraw their minds from the external world."[7] The yogic pose emulating the tortoise is called kúrmakásana.

Over the years numerous postures exercising various organs and gland were developed. From all of these, Ánandamúrti has selected around forty that are useful in spiritual development as well as important in curing and preventing different diseases. (See Ánanda Márga Caryácarya Part 3 and *Yogic Treatments and Natural Remedies*).

The most important effect of ásanas is on the endocrine glands, which secrete hormones directly into the blood stream. The

7   *Ananda Marga Caryácarya Part 3.*

endocrine glands include the pancreas, thymus, thyroid, para-thyroid, adrenals and reproductive glands (testes and ovaries). If the secretion of any gland is too much or too little, then there will be a malfunctioning in the body. For example, if the thyroid gland, located in the throat, secretes too much fluid, a person will become thin. If the gland secretes too little fluid the person will become fat. The reason is that thyroxin, the hormone secreted by this gland, regulates metabolism or the rate in which the body converts food into energy. Ásanas can correct the malfunctioning of the thyroid and other glands by putting pressure on the gland, which in effect massages the gland and regulates the amount of blood flowing to that gland.

Ásanas also help to keep the spinal cord flexible, which is important in retarding the effects of aging on the body. As people grow older the spinal column usually becomes rigid. Proper per-formance of ásanas can prevent this.

Another important effect of ásanas is that they help various organs of the body to function properly. For example, there are several ásanas that massage the stomach and intestines and other organs involved in digestion and the elimination of wastes. Problems such as indigestion, constipation, gastric ulcers, liver malfunction, etc., can be checked and corrected by performing certain ásanas in combination with a proper diet.

According to Ánanda Márga yoga, yoga postures should be selected for the student by a teacher who is able to prescribe the ásanas needed by that individual. Although there are numerous ásanas, everyone has a unique physical structure with different strengths and weaknesses, so certain ásanas may be more suited to one person than to another. In choosing the ásanas, the yoga teacher (Ácárya) will also consider the effect of the ásanas on the subtle nervous centers of the body — the *cakras*).

There are two subtle nerves running up the trunk of the body crisscrossing each other five times at the spinal column. Where these nerves cross are centers of psychic energy known as cakras (pronounced chakras). These cakras are not anatomical organs but they control the functioning of the various organs in the region adjacent to the chakra. Thus a person suffering from respiratory problems will need ásanas that strengthen the cakra at the center of the chest. To overcome digestive problems, ásanas that exercise the cakra at the navel region will be required. The diagram below shows the location of the cakras and organs and the basic factors that they control. A more complete description of the cakras is provided in the next chapter.

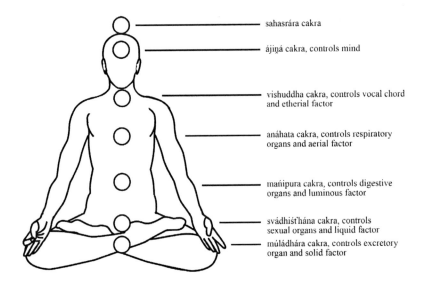

sahasrára cakra

ájiṇá cakra, controls mind

vishuddha cakra, controls vocal chord and etherial factor

anáhata cakra, controls respiratory organs and aerial factor

maṅipura cakra, controls digestive organs and luminous factor

svádhiśt'hána cakra, controls sexual organs and liquid factor

múládhára cakra, controls excretory organ and solid factor

DIAGRAM 1: THE CAKRAS

In addition to helping to bring about physical well-being, the ásanas have an important effect on the mind. When glandular functions are well balanced this contributes to mental balance. Also, by strengthening the psychic centers the ásanas help control the mental propensities (vrttis) controlled by these centers. These fifty mental propensities are distributed in the six lower chakras.

The fourth component of Aśtáuṇga Yoga is *práńáyáma* or control of vital energy. Práńáyáma is a well-known practice of yoga, usually described as "breath control" but the principle upon which this practice is based is less well known and deserves explanation. Tantra defines life as the parallelism of physical and mental waves in proper coordination with vital energies. The vital energies are known as *váyus* or winds. There are ten váyus in the human body that are responsible for various activities, including respiration, blood circulation, excretion of wastes, movement of limbs, etc. The controlling point of these váyus is an "organ" known as *práńendriya* (like the cakras, práńendriya is not an anatomical structure). This práńendriya also links the various sensory organs with a point in the brain. The práńendriya is located in the center of the chest and it pulsates in synchronization with the process of respiration. When there is a rapid pulsation of the breath and the práńendriya, it is more difficult for the mind to link up with sensory perceptions. For example, if you run a race of one thousand meters you cannot immediately eat something and recognize the flavor of what you have eaten due to rapid breathing and the disturbed functioning of the práńendriya. During rapid breathing it also becomes more difficult to concentrate the mind.

In práńáyáma there is a special process of breathing in which the pulsation of the práńendriya becomes still and the mind becomes calm. This helps meditation greatly. Práńáyáma also readjusts the balance of vital energy in the body. Práńáyáma is a complicated practice and can be dangerous if not taught and guided by a competent teacher. The practitioner of práńáyáma must maintain a spiritual thought in the mind while doing the exercise—if not, his or her mind may focus on a negative propensity (such as anger, for example) and the mind will become degraded rather than elevated. It is also important to know in which part of the body the vital energy should be concentrated. Because of these complexities práńáyáma is usually taught following a preparatory period in which the student becomes familiar with the basic meditation process and other practices. In the system of Ánanda Márga yoga evolved by Shrii Shrii Ánandamúrti, práńáyáma is the fourth lesson in a series of six lessons of meditation techniques taught individually to students as they become ready for successive lessons.

The fifth limb of Aśtáuṇga Yoga is known as *pratyáhára*, which means "to withdraw the mind from its attachment to external objects." In Tantra the repetition of mantra is preceded by a process in which the meditator directs his or her mind to one point. The stories of yogis who are so deep in meditation that they cannot even feel pins being stuck into their bodies are examples of the efficacy of this practice. However, it is not an easy matter to arrive at such a state of sensory withdrawal. After constant and regular practice, a beginning meditator can gradually gain success in this process.

Another part of pratyáhára is called "the offering of colors." Each vibration in the universe has a color associated with it, and for every object of the mind there is an associated vibration and color. During meditation one's mind may be occupied with different objects. At the end of meditation, the meditator visualizes and symbolically offers to the Supreme Consciousness the colors associated with the thoughts that have disturbed the mind during meditation. Through this process the mind becomes detached from these thoughts and objects. This lesson of offering the colors is taught as part of the second lesson of individual instruction in the Ánanda Márga system of Tantra yoga.

The sixth limb of Aśtáuṇga Yoga is *dháraná*. Dháraná is the concentration of the mind at a specific point. In the basic lesson of Tantric meditation the aspirant brings his or her mind to a specific cakra, which is his or her spiritual and psychic nucleus. This point (called the *iśṭa* cakra) varies from person to person and is indicated by the teacher of meditation at the time of initiation. When the mind is well concentrated on the point, then the process of repeating the mantra begins. If the concentration is lost, the aspirant must again bring his or her mind back to the point of concentration. This practice of bringing one's mind to the point of concentration is a form of dháraná.

In addition to this dháraná found in the first lesson of meditation, there is another form of dháraná known as *tattva dháraná* in which the aspirant concentrates on the cakras and the specific factors controlled by the cakras. This lesson is important because it helps the meditator to gain control over the mental propensities governed by that cakra as well as to increase the concentration powers of the mind, which is especially valuable in the other lessons of meditation. Tattva dhárańá also has the effect of loosening the pressure of the *ida* and *piuṇgala* (pronounced pin-gah-lah) channels on the *suśumna* channel. When this pressure is loosened, the spiritual energy (kulakuńḍalinii) can flow more easily upward. Tattva dhárańá is taught as the third lesson of this series of Tantra Yoga.

When someone has gained skill in dhárańá, he or she can then learn the seventh limb of Aśtáuṇga Yoga, which is *dhyána*. In this process, the mind is first brought to a particular cakra and then is directed in an unbroken flow toward the Supreme Consciousness. This flow continues until the mind becomes completely absorbed in the Supreme Consciousness. This process is difficult and is only given after the aspirant has practiced all the preceding steps, particularly dhárańá.

There are different forms of dhyána, and through the study of dhyána we can understand the relationship of Tantra with other spiritual traditions. When Tantric teachers from India first brought this form of meditation to China, it became known as Chan, and when Chan was brought to Japan via Korea, it finally became known as Zen. Although there are important differences between contemporary Zen meditation and the dhyána as practiced by the Tantric masters in India, the root teaching was the same. Dhyána helps to perfect the most subtle layer of the mind and leads the person to the final step of Aśtáuṇga Yoga, which is *samádhi*.

Samádhi is not like the other seven steps in that it is not a particular method or practice; rather it is the result of practicing the other parts of Aśtáuṇga Yoga. It is the absorption of mind in the Supreme Consciousness. There are two principal forms of samádhi: *nirvikalpa* and *savikalpa*. Savikalpa is a trance of absorption with distortion or qualification. In savikalpa samádhi the person has the feeling "I am the Supreme Consciousness," but in nirvikalpa samádhi there is no longer a feeling of "I." The individual consciousness is totally merged in the Cosmic Consciousness.

Those who experience this state are not able to explain or describe it because it occurs when the mind has ceased to function. The only way they can even know that they experienced this state is after the mind leaves this trance of absorption. Then they experience waves of extreme happiness and can assume that they were in the state of *nirvikalpa* samádhi. The attainment of samádhi comes after long practice in this life, or as a result of much practice in a previous life or through the grace of the guru. It is the culminating point in millions of years of development from lower forms of life to human and finally to merger with the source of all being.

Chapter 4

CAKRAS AND THE SUBTLE ANATOMY OF YOGA

A key to understanding how the mind, body and soul are connected lies in an appreciation of the psychic and spiritual structure of the human body.

The early Tantric yogis did mental experiments in which they meditated on the internal nature of mind and body. They observed that along the backbone of the body there is a nerve that is criss-crossed by two other subtle nerves. I use the word "subtle" because these are not physical nerves that can be seen in a dissection of a physical body. They do have psychic and spiritual existence, though.

The nerve running up the center is called the *suśumna* and the nerve on the left side is called *ida* and the right side is called *piuṇgala*. Wherever the two nerves cross over the central suśumna nerve we find a special area called a cakra (pronounced and often spelled as chakra).

Cakra means "circle" and these centers are roughly circular in shape, though as we will see they have particular individual characteristics. The cakras are also sometimes called lotuses because around the circular shape the yogis observed petals. Inside the circles there are shapes and the shapes have unique colors.

The cakras are important points of the body because the first five cakras control the fundamental factors (solid, liquid, luminous and aerial) that compose the body as well as the five basic layers of the mind. In fact, Ánandamúrti defines cakras as "the different seats of the mind for controlling the fundamental factors."[8]

The cakras are associated with glands that secrete hormones that affect the mind and body, which is of great importance in yoga. The first six cakras are linked with the glands that control fifty basic mental propensities, and each of the petals in these cakras is the controlling point for one propensity. In Sanskrit a mental propensity is termed *vrtti* (pronounced vri-ti). Because of this glandular link, the cakras play a major role in the proper functioning of the physical organs and nerves that lie in proximity to these centers. The science of yoga postures is based on this knowledge.

Let's look at the cakras:

Múládhára Cakra

---

8   Shrii Shrii Ánandamúrti, "This World and the Next," published in *Subhasita Samgraha 4.*

The first cakra is located in the first vertebra of the spinal column. It is called *múládhára*, which means "fundamental base." Inside the circular area of the cakra, the yogis observed a square shape with a golden yellow color. The first cakra is the controlling point of the solid factor in the human body.

The circular area is surrounded by four petals. Each of the four petals surrounding the circle governs a propensity and taken together these propensities constitute the four basic urges of a human being. The propensities governed by this chakra are:

1. Dharma - psycho-spiritual longing
2. Artha - psychic longing
3. Káma – physical longing
4. Mokśa – spiritual longing

This cakra is also the controlling point of the conscious mind (kámamaya kośa).

Svádhiśthána Cakra

The second cakra is located on the spinal column on a level plane with the root of the sex organ. This cakra is called *svádhisthána* cakra and its name means "seat of my own energy." Inside the circular area the ancient yogis observed a white crescent moon-shaped figure. This cakra controls the liquid factor in the body and the subconscious mind (*manomaya kośa*).

Surrounding the circular area there are six petals and each petal controls a particular propensity. The propensities of the second cakra are:

1. Avajiṇá – indifference
2. Múrcchá – psychic stupor, lack of common sense
3. Prashraya – indulgence
4. Avishvása – lack of confidence
5. Sarvanásha – thought of sure annihilation
6. Krurata – cruelty

The ovaries and testes are the physical glands associated with this cakra.

Mańipura Cakra

The third cakra is located on the spine on a plane level with the navel. This cakra is called *mańipura* and it means "the treasure house of the devotee." Inside the circular area is a triangle with a blood-red color. The circular area is surrounded by ten petals. This cakra controls the luminous (fire) factor of the body as well as the first layer of the superconscious mind (*atimánasa kośa*).

The ten petals of the third cakra govern the following propensities:

1. Lajjá - shyness, shame
2. Pishunatá – sadistic tendency
3. Iirśá– envy
4. Suśupti – static state, sleepiness
5. Viśáda – melancholy
6. Kaśáya – peevishness
7. Trśńá – yearning for acquisition
8. Moha – infatuation
9. Ghrńá – hatred, revulsion
10. Bhaya – fear

The adrenal gland and the pancreas are associated with this cakra.

Anáhata Cakra

The fourth cakra is located on the spine at the level of the center of the chest. The fourth cakra is known as the *anáhata cakra*, which means "unstruck holy sound." It is also often referred to as the "heart center" or "heart cakra." Within the circular area of the cakra is a hexagon shape with a smoky grey-green color. The circular area is surrounded by twelve petals. This cakra controls the aerial (gaseous) factor of the human body as well as the second layer of the superconscious mind (*vijiṇánamaya kośa*).

The twelve petals of the cakra govern the following propensities:

1. Áshá, – hope
2. Cintá – worry
3. Ceśtá – effort
4. Mamatá – mine-ness, love
5. Dambha - vanity
6. Viveka – conscience, discrimination
7. Viklatá – mental numbness, due to fear
8. Ahaṁkara – ego
9. Lolatá– avarice
10. Kapaťatá – hypocrisy
11. Vitarka – argumentativeness to the point of exaggeration
12. Anutápa – repentance

The thymus gland is associated with this cakra.

Vishuddha Cakra

This cakra is located in the throat and its name means "spotless purity." Inside the circular area there is no particular form or fixed color, rather there are many points of various colors. This cakra controls the ethereal factor (medium through which sound travels) of the human body and the third layer of the superconscious mind (*hirańmaya kośa*).

The sixteen petals of this cakra govern the following propensities respectively:

1. Śadhaja – sound of peacock
2. Rśabha – sound of bull
3. Gándhára – sound of goat
4. Madhyama – sound of deer
5. Paiṇcama – sound of cuckoo
6. Dhaevata – sound of donkey
7. Niśáda – sound of elephant
8. Onm – acoustic root of creation, preservation and destruction, primordial sound

9. Hum – sound of arousing the kuṅdalinii
10. Phat– putting theory into practice
11. Vaośat – expression of mundane knowledge
12. Vasat – welfare in the subtler sphere
13. Sváhá – performing noble actions
14. Namah – surrender to the Supreme
15. Viśa – repulsive expression
16. Amrta – sweet expression

The first seven propensities of the Vishuddha cakra are sounds of animals. Based on these seven animal sounds, Shiva, the founder of Tantra, evolved the seven-note Indian scale (*surasaptaka*). This cakra is also the controller of the sound-carrying ethereal factor in the human body. With its mystical sound propensities and proximity to the vocal organ, it is indeed the focal point for all sonic expression in human beings. The thyroid and parathyroid glands are associated with this cakra.

Ájiṇa Cakra

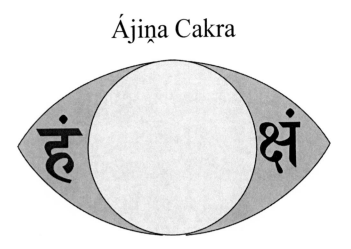

This cakra is located in the point between the eyebrows. Its Sanskrit name means "authority, command and unlimited power." This cakra is popularly known as the "third eye."

There is no form or fundamental factor associated with the ájiṇa cakra. This cakra is beyond form and color. It has two petals that are associated with mundane knowledge (*apará*) and spiritual knowledge (*pará*). This cakra is the seat or controlling point of the mind and is an important concentration point in meditation and advanced yogic practices.

The pituitary gland is associated with this cakra.

Sahasrára Cakra

This cakra is located at the crown of the head and is visualized as a lotus with one thousand petals. There are one thousand petals because the cakra controls all possible human expression. There are fifty propensities in the first six cakras. These propensities can function internally and externally and in ten different directions. Thus: 50 x 2 = 100 x 10 = 1000.

The pineal gland is the physical gland associated with this cakra.

The seven cakras described above are the cakras mentioned in most yogic texts and pictured in most diagrams of the cakras and the subtle nerves. In subtle yogic meditation there is another chakra situated just below the crown of the head. It is called guru cakra. Ánandamúrti says the guru cakra is the internal side of the sahasrára cakra and is situated below the pineal gland.

The cakra "map" pinpoints the controlling locations for important human urges and emotions and can be used to help people overcome psychic difficulties. For example, if someone has a fear of speaking in public, he or she could do yoga postures such as the peacock (*mayúrásana*) aimed at strengthening the third cakra. The propensities of shyness and fear are both located in the third cakra. Similarly other psychic problems can be addressed if one has a proper knowledge of the cakras and of yoga postures.

Acoustic Roots and Seed Mantras

In addition to controlling the elements of the body, mental propensities and particular layers of the mind, the cakras are also linked with particular sounds. Each cakra has a special seed (*biija*) mantra, and in most diagrams of the cakras that mantra is usually written in Devanagari script in the center of the cakra.

The seed mantras for the cakras are the acoustic roots of the particular element controlled by the cakra. An acoustic root is the fundamental sound associated with an idea, concept or action. According to Ánandamúrti, "Every vibration in this universe has color and sound. Every vibration also represents a particular idea, and hence each idea has a vibrational sound and vibrational color."[9] For example, if you are laughing you will make the sound "ha, ha, ha." The sound "ha, ha" is the root sound for the action of laughing. Similarly, the root sounds for each of the five elements (solid, liquid, luminous, aerial and ethereal) are the following *biija* mantras:

- Solid Factor (múládhára chakra): Laṁ (pronounced like the English word "lung")
- Liquid Factor (svádhiśthána chakra): Vaṁ (the "v" is pronounced like a "w")

---

9   Ánandamúrti, "The Acoustic Roots of the Indo-Aryan Alphabet," published in *Discourses on Tantra Volume 1*.

- Luminous Factor (maṇipura chakra): Raṁ (pronounced like English word "rung")
- Aerial Factor (anáhata chakra): Yaṁ (the "y" is pronounced as a "j" and the aṁ sound is pronounced like the "ung" in "hung")
- Etherial Factor (vishuddha chakra): Haṁ (pronounced like the English world "hung")

These root sounds are often shown in diagrams of the cakras and are used in advanced meditation lessons associated with the cakras.

In addition to these seed mantras for the five factors, there are other important sounds embedded in the cakras. As we have seen, each of the fifty petals in the first six cakras is associated with a gland that secretes a hormone that governs a particular human mental propensity. Each of these propensities has a corresponding root sound, and in some diagrams of the cakras, the letters for these sounds are written on the petals. These fifty sounds comprise the vowels and consonants of the Sanskrit alphabet.

Kuńdalinii: The Latent Divine Energy

Another important discovery of the early yogis is that at the base of the spine lies the *kuńdalinii*, or *kulakuńdalinii*. Kuńdalinii is the sleeping divine energy of the individual living being. The yogis say that it looks like a coiled snake, lying dormant in the first vertebra of the spinal cord. When the kuńdalinii is awakened by the repetition of an effective mantra it travels up the subtle nerve in the spinal column (*suśumná*) and as it goes through the different cakras the yogi experiences increasing degrees of proximity to the Supreme Consciousness.

When the kuńdalinii reaches the sahasrára cakra the spiritual aspirant merges with the Supreme Consciousness. This state is called nirvikalpa samadhi.

Ánandamúrti said, "The inner spirit of raising of the kulakuńdalinii is for one to control the [propensities] and seed sounds of the different glands and to suspend one's self in Paramashiva [the Nucleus Consciousness], whose rank is beyond the scope of all the instincts and seed sounds."[10]

---

10   Ánandamúrti, "Tantra and Its Effect on Society," published in *Discourses on Tantra, Volume 2.*

Chapter 5

KOŚAS: THE STRUCTURE
OF THE MIND

According to Ánanda Márga philosophy, the mind is pure consciousness that has been modified by the operative principle *(Prakrti)* to form three functional parts: *mahat* ("I am"), *aham* ("I do") and *citta* ("I have done").[11] However, due to the continued activity of the operative principle on the citta portion there is the creation of five different layers or *kośas*. In order to explain the intellectual and intuitional capabilities of the human being, it is important to understand the functioning of these five layers. In addition, understanding of the five layers of the mind also helps one in the various spiritual practices, which are designed to perfect these layers of the mind.

The division of the mind into five layers is similar to the structure of an onion—as one layer is peeled away the next layer is revealed until one reaches the innermost layer.

The outermost layer of the mind is actually the physical body, which we can consider to be the sixth layer of the mind. This physical body is formed from the food we eat and is known in

11   A fuller description of mahat, aham, citta appears in *Ananda Marga Elementary Philosophy*.

Sanskrit as *annamaya kośa.* By admitting that the body is the base of the mind, Ánanda Márga philosophy avoids the duality of mind and body that has troubled some philosophical systems. Also by accepting the body as an integral part of the mind, the practitioner of Tantra yoga includes the development of the body in the program of spiritual development.

The need to integrate a concern for the body in an overall program to develop the mind is demonstrated in the story of Gautama, the Buddha, who first tried to gain spiritual enlightenment by extreme austerities. After nearly starving to death, a young girl named Sujata brought him a bowl of rice-milk pudding and he regained his strength. He was then able to meditate properly and soon reached his goal.

Beyond the annamaya kośa we find the first non-physical layer of the mind, which is known as the kámamaya kośa. *Káma* signifies "desire" and it is this layer that controls and guides our relationship with the exterior world. The work of the sensory and motor organs (eyes, ears, nose, tongue, skin, limbs, etc.) is governed by this kośa. It is this layer of the mind that is at work during our normal waking consciousness. It senses the exterior world and helps our motor organs to react to the world. It is known in Western psychology as the "conscious mind." When someone sees a piece of cake he or she may desire to eat it. Finally, if his or her motor organs begin to carry out this desire, then we have a typical operation of the kamamaya kośa.

Going further into the mind we find another layer known as the manomaya kośa also known as the subtle mind. This is the layer that governs memory. All memory is stored here, and we can recall a previous experience due to the capacity of this layer. In addition, the mind's ability to process and use previously acquired data also depends on this layer.

An example of its operation is found in a university student who reads many books in preparation for an examination. At the time of the examination there may be one or two questions and it is the manomaya kośa that recollects the diverse facts from all the books and helps to synthesize them into a coherent response.

That is why the literal meaning of manomaya kośa is "the deep thinking layer of mind."

The manomaya kośa is known in psychology as the "subconscious mind." The subconscious mind is active during sleep while the conscious mind (kámamaya kośa) is inactive. Dreams take place in this layer. It is in the manomaya kośa where pain and pleasure are experienced.

Unlike many schools of Western psychology, Ánanda Márga philosophy states that the mind does not end with the subconscious layer. Beyond the manomaya kośa there are three layers that are collectively known as kárána mánas or "causal mind." Some psychologists, notably Carl Jung, have called this the "unconscious mind." This causal mind is concerned with the intuitive capabilities of the human being, but due to the constant activity of the conscious and subconscious minds, it is rarely experienced by most human beings. This is perhaps why its study has been neglected in most schools of psychology.

This causal mind has also been called the collective unconscious by Carl Jung because all the knowledge of past, present and future is lying in it. The information in the causal mind is not limited to the memory and experience of the individual, as is the data in the subconscious mind. It is because of the existence of this causal mind that we can explain the extraordinary experiences of prophets, psychics, clairvoyants and others who have predicted future events or who have known things beyond the limits of their sense organs.

An example is the case of the scientist Mendeleyev, who was the first person to formulate the periodic table of elements, an arrangement of the physical elements in order of their atomic weight. Mendeleyev was asked how he had determined this arrangement and he responded by explaining that one night he was dreaming and in his dream he saw the periodic table of the elements. He woke up and copied it down.

The American clairvoyant Edgar Cayce was able to diagnose the illnesses of people who were thousands of kilometers away from him. This is another example of the extraordinary capacity of the causal mind.

The Old Testament story of Joseph's dreams in which he predicted several years of good harvests followed by several years of famine in ancient Egypt is another example of the limitless knowledge that lies in the more subtle layers of mind.

Similarly, there is an Indian tale of a man who worshiped the goddess Kali in order to find a remedy for his sick child; subsequently he was told the proper medicine in a dream by the goddess. In these cases, the dreamers went into deep sleep in which they penetrated beyond the manomaya kośa into the causal mind.

In Ánanda Márga philosophy, three layers of the causal mind are recognized. The first layer is called atimánasa kośa. It is here where the desire for spiritual realization originates. The faculties of clairvoyance, intuition and artistic creativity are characteristic functions of this layer.

The second layer of the causal mind is vijináṇamaya kośa or "special-knowledge" kośa. Two of the most important intuitional qualities that humans can develop are expressed in this kośa. One is *viveka* or discernment, the ability to know what is permanent and what is transitory. The true sage knows that the passing show of this material world is only a relative truth and he or she is able to see the unchanging and absolute Consciousness behind the panorama of the physical world. When viveka is developed then the second quality, *vaeragya,* gets expression. Vaeragya is the renunciation of and non-attachment to transitory physical objects. It does not mean running away from worldly objects like a hermit in a cave but rather psychic nonattachment to objects. This state is best expressed in the story of India's legendary sage-king, Janaka, who is said to have remarked "even if my kingdom goes up in smoke, I have lost nothing."

The final layer of the causal mind is the hiránmaya kośa or "golden layer." In this kośa a practitioner of Tantra yoga can experience a brilliant, golden effulgence and experience the pure "I" feeling. When the aspirant reaches this layer, he or she has the awareness that only a thin veil separates him or her from the pure witnessing consciousness (atman) that lies beyond the kośas.

In this stage one has an intense desire to merge in the Supreme Consciousness. This is the realm of divine love. Shrii Shrii Ánandamúrti compares the mind to a mirror that can reflect the Cosmic Consciousness. He says that if the mirror is not clean then the reflection of consciousness is not clear. We can think of the kośas as the different layers of our mind's "mirror." If there are imperfections in the different layers, then the reflection of consciousness is not fully perceived, and we may be unaware that there is pure consciousness beyond our mind. That is why Tantra yoga utilizes the eight steps of Aśtáuṇga Yoga to purify each of the kośas.

The development of the mind can be accomplished by natural processes but it can be greatly accelerated by the application of the various yoga practices. The body or annamaya kośa is developed naturally through physical labor and exercise while yoga prescribes ásanas and the proper selection of food to develop the kośa.[12]

The development of the kámamaya kośa through natural means comes about due to physical clash—the struggle to live in the world. In Aśtáuṇga yoga the practice of yama and niyama helps one to develop the conscious mind by strengthening one's conscience. The manomaya kośa is also developed naturally through physical struggles and in yoga through the practice of práńáyáma. The atimánasa kośa, or first layer of the causal mind, is developed naturally through psychic clash, struggles in the realm of mind that everyone faces in the course of life. The yogic practice for the development of the atimánasa kośa is pratyáhára, the withdrawal of the senses from attachment to external objects.

The second layer of the causal mind, the vijiṇánamaya kośa, is likewise developed in all humans through psychic struggles and in yoga practice by the technique of dhárańa. Finally the development of the last kośa, hirańyamaya kośa, comes about in all humans due to their longing for the Infinite. In yoga the practice of dhyána develops this last and most subtle portion of the mind.

---

12   See the book *Food For Thought*, Ananda Marga Publications.

TABLE 1, DEVELOPMENT OF KOŚAS

Kośa (layer of the mind)	Yogic Means of Development	Natural Means of Development
Annamaya (physical body)	Asanas and food	Physical clash
Kámamaya (conscious mind)	Yama-Niyama	Physical clash
Manomaya (subconscious mind)	Práńáyáma	Physical clash
Atimánasa (supramental mind)	Pratyáhára'	Psychic clash
Vijiṇánamaya (subliminal mind)	Dhárańá	Psychic clash
Hiránmaya kośa (subtle causal mind)	Dhyána	Longing for the Great (spiritual yearning.)

Chapter 6

BRAHMACAKRA: THE COSMIC CYCLE

In all civilizations people have attempted to explain the origin of the world in one way or another. In each cultural group one can find some mythology in which the story of creation is explained. Most of these stories do not, however, agree with what modern science says about the universe. In Ánanda Márga philosophy one can find a theory about the origin of the universe that is not only in accord with the present views of modern science but can also serve to guide scientists in their quest to find the answers to the many cosmological questions that are as yet unresolved.

This Tantric view of cosmology, while scientific, is also profoundly spiritual. The wonder of how the stars move precisely in their orbits, the intricacy and beauty of the various living creatures from amoeba to human and other evidence of a profound intelligence and order in the universe are not neglected by the Tantric conception of creation and development of the cosmos. Rather, Ánanda Márga cosmology begins by looking to the Infinite Consciousness that is the source of everything. This Consciousness is considered to be the first cause and is known as Brahma. Thus the cycle of creation in which Brahma transforms itself into this manifested universe is known as Brahmacakra.

Brahma means "the Entity that is great and has the capacity to make others great." Brahma is composed of consciousness and energy. In Sanskrit, consciousness is known as *puruśa* and energy is called *prakrti*. (Another name for consciousness is Shiva, and energy can also be called Shakti). Although we can say that Brahma is a composite of consciousness and energy, it must be emphasized that Brahma is a singular entity. These two "parts" are like the two sides of a piece of paper—they can never be separated. Consciousness never exists independently from the cosmic energy.

Just what exactly is consciousness? Puruśa or consciousness can be defined according to the various functions it performs. First of all, consciousness performs the act of witnessing all events of the universe. It is like a chandelier hanging in a room from the ceiling; many different actions take place under the witnessing light bulb, but the light bulb itself does not undergo change or participate directly in the action it witnesses. It provides the light that makes all the activities possible and "observes" all the activities. It is the cognitive faculty.

Another function of consciousness is that it is the material cause of the universe. It is the basic "stuff" from which everything else is composed. Scientists have always been searching to find the fundamental matter of the universe. At one time they thought that the atom was the smallest particle, but in recent years they have been dividing and subdividing the atom, finding smaller particles with no end in sight. Yogis have long said that the ultimate cause of existence and the source of all material objects is nothing but pure consciousness.

Still another way to describe consciousness is by saying that it is the "efficient cause" of the universe. It is the fundamental entity controlling all actions in this universe. Consciousness is like the master architect who has made the plan of the universe and acts to carry it out.

However, the architect takes the help of prakrti, the operative principle, in order to carry out his task. Prakrti is the other aspect of Brahma, the other side of the piece of paper, so to speak. In the cycle of creation the dominant and controlling role belongs to consciousness and the operative principle is considered to be a characteristic of consciousness. It is consciousness that permits the operative principle to work. If consciousness does not give the operative principle a chance to work, then the pure consciousness remains without any modification. In this condition, consciousness is beyond human conception because it does not have attributes such as form, smell, shape or color. Ánanda Márga philosophy calls this state of pure consciousness *Nirguńa Brahma*.

If the operative principle is given a chance to act, it works according to three fundamental modes. That is, prakrti creates differences in this world by modifying the original pure consciousness in three distinctive ways. These three fundamental styles of action are known as *guńas* in Sanskrit, a term which literally means "binding quality." This term derives from the idea that prakrti is like a rope that modifies the consciousness by binding it. When a particular guńa is active, there is a modification or bondage of the consciousness. The three guńas of prakrti are called *sattva* (sentient), *rajoguńa* (mutative), and *tamoguńa* (static).

Sattvaguńa creates the most subtle bondage or modification of the consciousness. It is responsible for the feeling of existence — 'I exist". Rajoguńa is responsible for the feeling "I do" and tamoguńa creates the feeling of "I have done". Tamoguńa works to objectify thought and is responsible for the creation of the solid objects that we observe in the universe, as will be shown below.

What is the process by which prakrti takes action and begins to modify the consciousness, creating *Saguńa Brahma* or Brahma with qualities? First, we must try to conceive of a state prior to the creation of the universe. Here the Supreme Consciousness is without any modification. The three guńas of prakrti exist but they are not active. If the three forces are represented by countless lines, the intersections of these lines form countless polygons. This is a theoretical way to picture the state in which consciousness is unmodified.

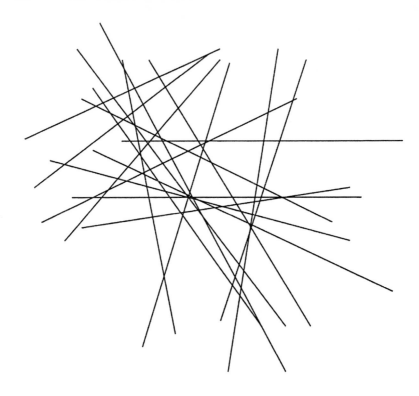

DIAGRAM 1: CAUSAL MATRIX

Going further, the most stable figure formed by the three forces is a triangle. In this "triangle of forces," the three guṅas are whirling around, transforming themselves, one into the other. Puruśa (consciousness) is "trapped" inside this triangle. The formation of this triangle signals the beginning of the creation of the universe. The puruśa inside the triangle is the nucleus of the universe, *Puruśottama*, and when the balance of forces in the triangle breaks down, one force, the sentient force, breaks out of the triangle and modifies consciousness.

This first modification of consciousness is very subtle. The feeling of "I exist" is created and consciousness becomes aware of itself. This "I exist" is called *mahattattva* and is the first portion of the Cosmic Mind. Following the first modification, the next force, rajoguṅa, becomes active and adds another quality to consciousness. The thought "I do" arises in the pure consciousness and the second part of the Cosmic Mind, *ahaṁtattva*, is created. Finally, the third guṅa, the static force or tamoguṅa, becomes active and further modifies consciousness. It gives the feeling "I have done." It objectifies consciousness by creating the third part of the Cosmic Mind, known as *citta* or mind-stuff.

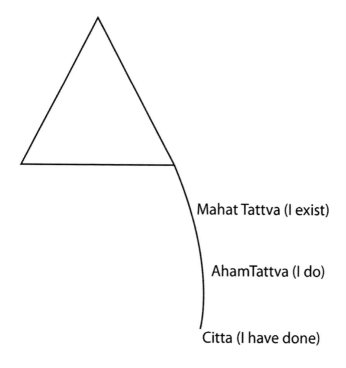

Mahat Tattva (I exist)

AhamTattva (I do)

Citta (I have done)

DIAGRAM 2: FORMATION OF THE COSMIC MIND

This description of the Cosmic Mind may seem abstract, but if we understand the functioning of our own mind, which is a small version of the Cosmic Mind, we can understand it better. If we see a tall tree, for example, what is actually happening? Our sense organs are receiving reflected light from the tree and this is transmitted to the brain and finally an image is formed in our mind. However, we can also close our eyes and still bring the image of the tree in our mind. The portion of the mind that gives the command to "create" the tree in the mind is the "I do" factor or ahamtattva, which is dominated by the mutative rajoguńa. The portion of the mind that forms the image of the tree is the citta or "I have done" factor. The citta is like a screen on which images are formed according to the commands of the "I do" factor. And in all the operations of the mind, the "I exist" or mahattattva must be present, because without a sense of "I" there cannot be any "I do."

Thus the Cosmic Mind functions in the same way as our individual minds, but there is an important difference that should be noted here. As we discussed above, the physical world (such as the tall tree) appears as an external reality to us, but for the Cosmic Mind the entire universe is an internal image in the vast cosmic citta. Also, in our individual minds if we use our imaginative power to create a green elephant, this image is not a reality for anyone except the one who imagined it. But if there is any image in the citta of the Cosmic Mind it is a reality and will be perceived as such by the microcosmic unit minds.

After the formation of the three parts of the Cosmic Mind, the static force (tamoguńa) continues to modify the citta portion of the Cosmic Mind and adds further attributes to the pure consciousness. It begins to transform a portion of the citta into the five fundamental factors.

In different ancient systems of thought there were said to be basic elements out of which all matter was composed. The ancient Greeks talked of earth, air, water and fire and in esoteric systems such as astrology these elements are also mentioned.

In the Ánanda Márga philosophy there are five fundamental factors. The first is known as ethereal factor or ákásha tattva. Although modern science abandoned the concept of ether after the Michelson-Morley experiments of the nineteenth century failed to detect it, we can reconcile the yogic system's ákásha tattva with modern science by thinking of it as "space-time." In Tantra this spatial factor is said to be able to carry the subtle primordial vibration known as onḿkára or om.[13]

13   Om is sound, but the word sound is used in a sense that is wider than the conventional definition in physics. For a more complete explanation see *Subhásita Saṁgraha* III, pp. 58-60.

As the tamoguṅa continues to modify consciousness, a portion of consciousness is transformed into *vayu tattva* or gaseous factor. This factor can carry sound and touch vibrations. The next factor is *tejas tattva* or luminous factor. This factor can carry sound, touch and sight vibrations. Following the luminous factor there is the creation of the liquid factor, *apa tattva*, which carries taste vibration as well as sound, touch and sight. The last factor, solid or *kṣiti tattva*, carries the smell vibration as well as the vibrations carried in the other factors. Thus, all things of this physical world exist in the citta of the Cosmic Mind and this material world can be considered a thought projection of the Cosmic Consciousness. Modern science is also moving toward this position. Physicist Sir James Jeans wrote, "The stream of knowledge is heading toward a nonmechanical reality; the universe begins to look more like a great thought than like a great machine."[14] Another physicist, Sir Arthur Eddington said:

The final realization that physical science is concerned with a world of shadows is one of the most significant advances. In the world of physics we watch a shadowgraph performance of the drama of familiar life. The shadow of my elbow rests on the shadow table as the shadow ink flows over the shadow paper. It is all symbolic, and as a symbol the physicist leaves it. Then comes the alchemist Mind who transmutes the symbols... to put the conclusion... The stuff of the world is mind stuff.[15]

When consciousness has been transformed into solid factor, one half of the cosmic cycle has been completed. The first part of the cosmic cycle, in which consciousness is transformed into Cosmic Mind and then into the five fundamental factors, is known as *saincara*, or "movement away from the cosmic nucleus." In the second half of the cycle, matter is transformed back into pure consciousness. This movement toward the nucleus of the universe is known as *pratisaincara*.

---

14   James Jeans, *The Mysterious Universe* (New York, The Macmillan Company, 1980).
15   Arthur Eddington, *The Nature of the Physical World* (New York; The Macmillan Company, 1928).

Previously we saw that through the action of the three guńas or binding principles consciousness is transformed into Cosmic Mind and that a portion of the Cosmic Mind is transformed into the basic elements that form the universe. The process of creation does not stop with the transformation of consciousness into inanimate objects. The binding principles of prakrti continue to transform consciousness and the development of animate beings is accomplished in this process.

It is the static principle of tamoguńa of prakrti that continues the relentless transformation of consciousness. At the end of the saincara phase we find the creation of solid factor. Tamoguńa puts pressure on the solid objects, attempting to compress them or to lessen the space between the molecules. This compression of the static principle causes the creation of forces within the object. One force in the object is called an "exterial" force, as it is moving outward from the center of the object, acting to break up the object. Another force may be termed "interial," as it moves toward the object's nucleus and acts to hold the object together.

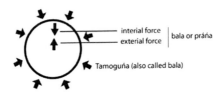

DIAGRAM 3: THE CREATION OF PRÁŃA

The collective name of these two forces is pránáh. If the center-seeking force is stronger, a nucleus is formed in the solid factor and this nucleus controls the pránáh or vital force in the object, giving rise to the possibility for the development of life. However, if the outer-seeking force is stronger, then a resultant force bursts the object apart. In Sanskrit this bursting apart of the crude factor is known as *jadasphoía*—the explosions of dying stars known to astronomers as supernova are examples of jadasphota. In jadasphota the solid factor is broken down into liquid, aerial, luminous and ethereal factors.

If, however, a nucleus is created in the object and the vital forces are controlled by a nucleus and if there is a congenial atmosphere in which there is a balance of the fundamental factors, then we can witness the first expression of life.[16]

With the creation of life we find an important event in the cosmic cycle. In each living entity there is a mind. The simpler the entity is in physical structure, the simpler will be its mind. Conversely, the more complex an entity's physical structure, the more complex will be its mind.

We may ask, what is the origin of the mind in the individual living being? Ánanda Márga philosophy says that within solid objects two forces are created under the pressure of the static force. As a result of friction caused by the conflict of these forces within the object, some portion of the solid is pulverized into something subtler, which is mind-stuff or citta. As the solids originated from mind (the Cosmic Mind), it is quite consistent and logical to say that unit or individual minds have come out of matter, because matter has come from mind and thus mental potentiality is inherent in all matter.

In one-celled living beings the mind is very simple. For example, in a protozoan, we can see that its behavior is reflexive or instinctive. If you put a hot needle next to it, it darts away automatically. This type of reflexive behavior is controlled by its simple mind, which is completely composed of citta. The sense of "I do" and "I exist" does not find expression in unicellular beings.

Life is in a state of evolution. Due to conflict and cohesion, simple animals and plants become more complex. In Ánanda Márga philosophy we also make the observation that tamoguńa, which has dominated the cycle of creation from the point of cosmic citta up to the point of creation of simple life, loses its

16   P. R. Sarkar's *Microvitum in a Nutshell* (Calcutta: Ananda Marga Publications, 1987) sheds new light on the subject by advancing the idea that the microvitum, subatomic particles with characteristics of living beings, are the first expressions of life. Chapter 7 in this book gives an overview of the Microvita concept.

dominance at this stage. Rajoguṅa, or the mutative force, now becomes dominant. In this stage, living beings become more and more physically developed and also their minds become more complex. Animals and plants have not only a mind that governs instinctive and reflexive behavior,but they also have the second functional part of the mind—the "I do" factor (ahaṁtattva).

When there is a significant portion of "I do" factor (also known in psychology as "ego") and it is greater in quantity than the citta portion of the mind that governs instinct, the animal has the capacity for intelligent behavior. In many animals we can see the beginning of intellect. They can learn by trial and error, for example, to avoid those things that give pain and to seek those things that give pleasure. As ahaṁtattva gets more developed, the behavior of animals becomes more complex.

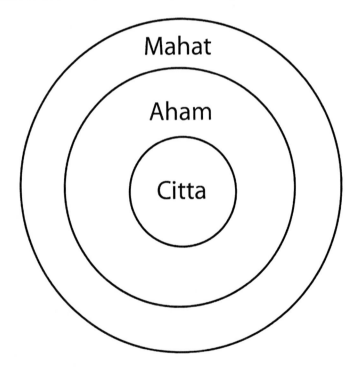

DIAGRAM 4: THE COMPOSITION OF THE MIND

Evolution continues, and in some animals and plants there is also the expression of another part of the mind. This further evolution of the mind is caused by the increasing activity of the most subtle and strongest guńa, sattvaguńa. The influence of sattvaguńa brings about the creation of the "I exist" factor (mahattattva). If the amount of mahattattva in a being's mind is greater than the amount of ahaṁtattva, the surplus portion is responsible for the creation of the intuitive faculty.

Whereas intellect is an analytical faculty, intuition is a synthetic faculty. With intellect we can know something by examining its parts whereas with intuition it is possible to know something in its entirety, in a holistic manner. Human beings who possess developed intuition are recognized as sages. Two important characteristics found among people with developed intuition are *viveka* (discernment) and *vaerágya* (non-attachment).

In the returning phase (pratisaiṇcara) of the cosmic cycle we have seen the evolution of life from simple to complex forms. Looking at the diagram of the Brahmacakra we can see that the cycle is oval shaped and not circular. This means that the speed of evolution near the top is greater. When the stage of human life is reached a crucial point is attained. Humans have the capacity to increase the speed of their evolution toward the nucleus of the cycle. This can be done through meditation. In meditation there is a process in which the citta (I have done) is merged into the ahaṁtattva (I do) and the aham is absorbed into the mahattattva (I exist). Because of this process, the intuition becomes greatly developed and that is why meditation is also known as the intuitional science.

When the mind, in the course of meditation, becomes transformed into this intuitional mahattattva and then merges with the Cosmic Mind, one experiences the state known as savikalpa samádhi. The meditator at this time feels "I am one with the cosmic consciousness." But this is not the ultimate state. When the whole mind is dissolved into the witnessing consciousness there is a state known as nirvikalpa samádhi. In this state there is no feeling of "I", and hence no self-consciousness, only ecstatic union.

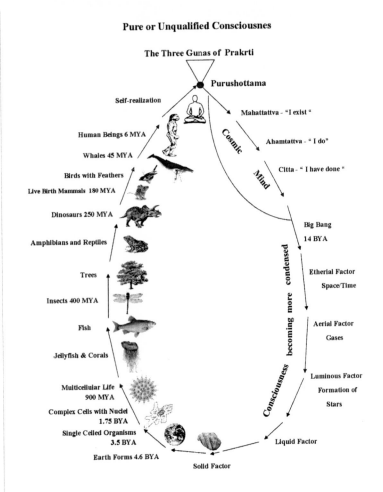

Pure or Unqualified Consciousnes

The Three Gunas of Prakrti

Purushottama

Self-realization

Mahattattva - "I exist "

Human Beings 6 MYA

Ahamtattva - " I do"

Whales 45 MYA

Citta - " I have done "

Birds with Feathers

Live Birth Mammals 180 MYA

Big Bang
14 BYA

Dinosaurs 250 MYA

Amphibians and Reptiles

Etherial Factor
Space/Time

Trees

Insects 400 MYA

Aerial Factor
Gases

Fish

Jellyfish & Corals

Luminous Factor
Formation of
Stars

Multicellular Life
900 MYA

Complex Cells with Nuclei
1.75 BYA

Single Celled Organisms
3.5 BYA

Liquid Factor

Earth Forms 4.6 BYA

Solid Factor

Cosmic Mind

Consciousness becoming more condensed

DIAGRAM 5: BRAHMACAKRA : THE COMIC CYCLE

What is the final destiny of life? Yoga is said to be the union of the individual consciousness with the nucleus of the cosmic cycle. In Ánanda Márga philosophy, this union is described in another way. Rather than merging with the nucleus of the cosmic cycle, the goal is to merge with the undifferentiated pure consciousness (Nirguńa Brahma), which exists beyond the manifested universe (Saguńa Brahma). Permanent union with Nirguńa Brahma is known as *mokśa*.

To attain mokśa Shrii Shrii Ánandamúrti introduces a unique concept—*Táraka Brahma.* According to Ánanda Márga philosophy, Brahma exists as the manifested universe (saguńa) and another infinite portion of Brahma remains beyond the influence of the operative principle and is undifferentiated (nirguńa). The link between the manifested and unmanifested Brahma is Táraka Brahma, which means Brahma, the liberator. If a tangent is drawn touching the ellipse that we used to represent Saguńa Brahma (see diagram 6), the tangential point is a point that is both inside and outside the ellipse.

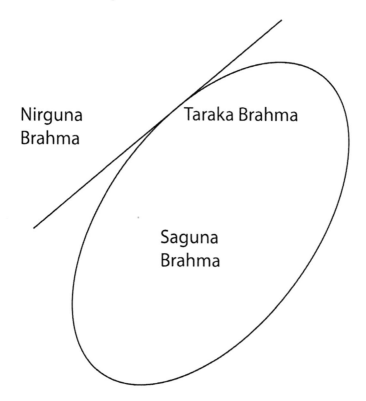

Nirguna
Brahma

Taraka Brahma

Saguna
Brahma

DIAGRAM 6: TÁRAKA BRAHMA

This point is both saguńa and also nirguńa. It is Táraka Brahma. The great spiritual teachers who appear from time to time in human history are embodiments of this tangential entity whose role is to guide individuals to complete self-realization and ultimate union with Nirguńa Brahma. The concept of Táraka Brahma is a devotional concept and explains the reverence that is given to great spiritual masters.

When individuals merge their unit consciousness with the Supreme Unmanifested Consciousness we have the completion of Brahmacakra. However, as one unit is liberated, new matter is constantly being created. Saguńa Brahma goes on for infinite time. The thought projection of the Cosmic Mind can never stop. This means that the universe is indestructible and eternal.

Reviewing Brahmacakra we can see that points of scientific, religious and even political controversies are enlightened by this view of the universe. For example the Judeo-Christian religion says that "man was made in the image of God." What does this mean? Is God a man in the sky with a big beard? This is not acceptable to logic, but we can say that the mind of humans, having all of the three functional parts (citta, aham and mahat), is a replica or a reflection of the Cosmic Mind.

Turning to scientific inquiry, Brahmacakra offers interesting perspectives on some questions that contemporary physics is trying to answer. Did the universe begin with a big bang? Is new matter being constantly created? Does the universe have a shape? Studying the universe through the perspective of Brahmacakra we see that matter is being constantly created. In some of his writings Ánandamúrti has said that the universe, although very vast, is not infinite and does have a shape, which conforms to the physicists' findings that space has curvature.

Finally, more and more physicists have seen the difficulty in finding the base of all things and have reached the same conclusions as the ancient philosophers. The atom, once thought to be the smallest and ultimate particle, has been subdivided into smaller particles and more and more subatomic particles are still being discovered. That is why some thinkers have already come to the conclusion that the base of matter and energy is consciousness itself. Sir James Jeans said that reality is better described as "mental rather than material."

Brahmacakra even sheds light on competing social theories. Many materialists argue that mind is a creation of matter and that matter is the most important element in all considerations of society. Ánandamúrti's theory agrees that unit minds have come out of matter but contends that this was only possible because matter has come out of Cosmic Mind and mind is thus inherent in matter. Ultimately, consciousness is the most important aspect of the universe.

Brahmacakra also gives another perspective on an important philosophical question. Is the universe an illusion or a reality, and what should be our approach to the material world? Some philosophers have said that this world is only an illusion and for a long time the lack of material advancement in India and other parts of Asia was in part due to the influence of this kind of philosophy. Ánandamúrti contends that this manifested universe is a relative reality because it is constantly changing. Nirguńa Brahma, on the other hand, is an absolute unchanging reality. However, we are part of this relative reality and we cannot deny its existence without also denying our own existence. Shrii Shrii Ánandamúrti thus advises that we should maintain an objective adjustment with the material world, carrying out our social obligations, but at the same time we should make the Supreme Consciousness the goal of our life and move toward union with this blissful consciousness.

Chapter 7

MICROVITA AND THE MYSTERY OF LIFE

In the previous chapter we have seen how pure consciousness is transformed into Cosmic Mind and then how the Cosmic Mind is transformed into the basic rudimental factors of the physical and perceivable universe. Furthermore, at a certain point, due to the continued activity of prakrti (the creative force of the Supreme Entity) living beings are formed from the solid factor.

On the last day of December 1986, Shrii Shrii Ánandamúrti elaborated on this process further by introducing the concept *of microvita* (literally, "small life"). He said that in the universe there are entities that straddle the line between mind and matter. These entities are situated somewhere between electrons and "ectoplasm" or mind-stuff. They are living entities and they, not carbon atoms or molecules, are the initial stage of life in the universe.

These microvita (microvitum is the singular term; in plural they are microvita) can be found in three basic sizes. The largest of the microvita are observable with the help of an extremely powerful microscope. Other, more subtle, microvita cannot be observed by any microscope, but could be perceived due to their "actional expression" or "actional vibration." Still more subtle are a class of microvita that Ánandamúrti says can only be perceived by a special kind of perception, "by persons having highly developed minds, having spiritually oriented minds."

According to Ánandamúrti, the largest kinds of microvita are the same entities that are commonly referred to as viruses, and that diseases that we say are caused by a virus are actually caused by microvita.

Another startling observation is that microvita move throughout the entire universe, traveling from one celestial body to another. Ánandamúrti said that they move through various media, including sound, smell, and touch. "The so-called virus of a diseased person moves through his or her sound," he noted.

Mentioning that microvita move through the universe, Ánandamúrti also stated that "these microvita are the carriers of life in different stars, planets and satellites — not carbon atoms or carbon molecules." And he added that "the root cause of life is not the unicellular protozoa or unit protoplasmic cell, but this unit microvitum."

Following the first discourse on microvita, Ánandamúrti gave several more in which he further described their characteristics and also suggested how the understanding of microvita could change chemistry, medicine and other fields of knowledge as well as the realm of spiritual practice.

Microvita and Science

People have often noticed that minerals with the same chemical composition sometimes vary according to where they are mined and where they were refined. Food preparations made in one kitchen may not taste the same when prepared with the same exact recipe in another kitchen. In the munitions industry it is observed that a firecracker manufactured in one plant may be louder than one made in another plant using the same formula. In the future, microvita theory may be able to explain these anomalies. Chemical formulas will be rewritten with the names of the atoms, like $H2O$, but also with an indication of the quantity and quality of microvita present in the substance.

Ánandamúrti also predicted that scientists of the future, equipped with knowledge of microvita, will be able to produce more effective medicines, fuels and fertilizers. As microvita is intimately connected with life and cellular protoplasm, future scientists will also be able to make advances in the medical and biological sciences based on their knowledge of microvita. The already astounding advances in genetics and related fields will be greatly accelerated when microvita are better understood.

Positive and Negative Microvita

Microvita are also important in the psychic and spiritual realms. Some microvita are very subtle and some are crude. Some have positive effects on humans and some have a negative impact on the human body and mind. Although Ánandamúrti coined the term "microvitum" in 1986, knowledge about this phenomenon is part of human folk wisdom stretching back into ancient times. In India positive microvita were known as *devayoni* or luminous bodies. In the West, tales of helpful leprechauns, pixies and fairies are perhaps also based on microvita. Similarly, negative microvita that attack the physical structures of people or have a negative influence on their mind were known as *pretayonis* in India, and in other places as elves, goblins and demons.

Devayonis, or collections of positive microvita, are composed of three factors—ethereal, luminous, and aerial—and do not have the solid or liquid factors. Here are some examples:

1. Gandharva : These are the microvita that arouse the love of the fine arts in the human mind. "They convey messages of the subtle world to human ears in this physical world, and by removing the darkness of crude ignorance, illuminate the human mind with a flood of divine effulgence." The mysterious muse that inspires artists and other creative people is another way to describe this type of positive microvita.

2. Kinnara: These are the microvita that "create a thirst for beauty — a strong desire for beautification and decoration." If these microvita help a person to direct his or her mind to the highest and most subtle kind of beauty, toward the cosmic realm, then they are positive. On the other hand, if they lead the mind toward matter then their effect is negative.

3. Vidyádhara: These are the microvita that "create a deep urge in the human mind to attain good qualities." Ánandamúrti explains that these microvita assist people who are trying to learn and to study. He even recounted an experience from his boyhood when he was a student. He said that he was studying for an examination and a sound came from all corners of his room. The sound implored him to learn certain lines from a particular poem by heart. The next day when he took his examination the same lines from that poem were part of the questions.

4. Siddha: These are considered to be the best of the luminous bodies as they "help in the domain of spirituality." They inspire humans to move on the path of spirituality and meditation. Without mentioning names, Ánandamúrti gave an example, saying that if there is a prince who is living in luxury and he suddenly gets an urge to become a monk and search for the cause of human misery, then this is an example of siddha microvita at work. This description fits the story of Buddha, who was a prince before becoming a great spiritual teacher.

Negative Microvita

In ancient India people believed that the minds of evil people could live on after their death and create woe for living human beings. These entities were called *pretayonis* or *gandhapishácas*. In the West there were similarly stories of goblins and evil spirits.

These tales can be understood in light of microvita theory. Just as positive microvita can inspire people to express themselves in a better way, various kinds of negative microvita can increase thoughts of depression, suicide, sadism, restlessness, inferiority and other debilitating tendencies.

A striking example of this is the category of negative microvita which is known as *kabandha*. Here is how Ánandamúrti describes them: "People who commit suicide due to humiliation, psychic distortion, frustration or the overpowering influence of excessive attachment, anger, greed, vanity, jealousy, etc. get the status of *kabandhayoni* after death. Wherever these entities happen to see other human beings under the spell of psychic derangement, they incite them to commit suicide."

Positive and negative microvita can also influence the physical health of a person and thus are important in medicine and healing. "There are certain persons who can cure diseases merely by touch. The science behind this is also the application of positive microvita." Elaborating further, Ánandamúrti said that in some cases "positive microvita eat the negative microvita."

Microvita and psycho-spiritual practice

The yogic study of the human body shows that there are fifty basic propensities. Some of the propensities seem to be positive and others negative. The practice of meditation (dhyána) attracts positive microvita and reduces the strength of the bad propensities. Ánandamúrti says, "Good propensities are enhanced by positive microvita and the bad propensities are reduced by positive microvita."

Positive microvita can help a person transform what could be a negative propensity into something positive. For example, the *avajiná* propensity of the second chakra is "indifference." If you are indifferent to something good, then this is a negative expression of this propensity and it can be caused by negative microvita. Similarly, if you are indifferent to something bad then this is a trait that is enhanced by the positive microvita and can help you from being ensnared in difficulty.

If we know that both positive microvita and negative microvita exist in the environment, then a logical question is how can we attract positive microvita and protect against negative microvita? Ánandamúrti said that the nature of our thoughts plays a big role in helping us to attract positive microvita.

A mind engaged in degenerating thought invites negative microvita. Good company, good books, good literature, good songs, kiirtanas (devotional chanting) elevate the mind and the mind becomes sanctified. That is why negative microvita do not get much scope to touch the mutative and sentient portions of the structure. [17]

Thus by following an uplifting way of life we can begin to harness the helpful influence of positive microvita and check the influence of the negative microvita that may be in the environment around us.

---

17 *Microvitum in a Nutshell.*

Chapter 8

LIFE, DEATH AND REBIRTH

What happens when a person dies? Is there anything after life? Is there a life prior to our existence in this body? These are questions that are inevitably asked when we begin to search for an understanding of our place in the universe. Ánanda Márga philosophy answers these questions systematically. However, in order to understand the response to these questions, it is necessary to understand the law of action and reaction.

In the physical realm there is a well-known law: for every action there is an equal and opposite reaction. In the mental sphere there is a similar law at work. Suppose Mr. A hits Mr. B and Mr. B responds by immediately hitting Mr. A with a force equal to the first punch. In this case the action was followed by an immediate reaction causing Mr. A to suffer a pain equal to that which he inflicted on Mr. B.

If we were to draw a diagram representing Mr. A's mind during this process of hitting and retaliation by Mr. B it would be as follows:

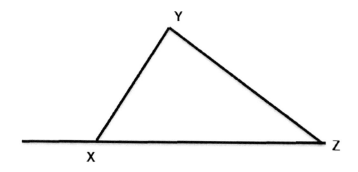

DIAGRAM 1:

Point X is the original state of Mr. A's mind before the action of hitting Mr. B. Point Y represents the distortion of his mind's plastic portion (citta). Every time there is any kind of action, good or bad, there is some distortion of the citta. Point Z represents the moment when Mr. A's mind returns to its original state. In this case it occurs as soon as Mr. B. makes his counter punch.

Whenever we make an action, our mind is distorted and when we experience the reaction, our mind returns to the original state and we feel either pleasure or pain depending on the nature of the original action. Many times, the process of action and reaction works like this. There is an action and immediately following it the person experiences the reaction. If there has been no change of time, place and person the reaction will be equal in strength to the original action.

However, there is another possibility. Suppose Mr. A hits Mr. B but the reaction is delayed. Mr. B doesn't respond with a punch. Five years later, however, Mr. A walks down a lonely street in a strange city and an unknown man appears and hits Mr. A many times. This is a delayed reaction experienced with an intensity exceeding that of the original action. This distortion of the mind that remains dormant for some time is known as *saṁskára* in Ánanda Márga philosophy. A saṁskára represents a reaction in potential form. In diagram 2 it appears as follows:

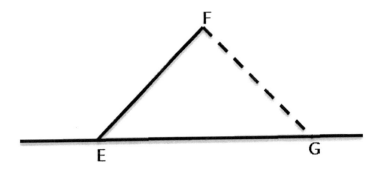

DIAGRAM 2 :

Line EF represents the original action and line FG represents the potential reaction (saṁskára) that can be experienced at any time. Thus, apparent accidents are simply reactions to previous actions. They sometimes appear to be without cause, but that is only because we have forgotten the original action. The reaction will be stronger than the original action if there is a passage of time between the two events and if there is a change in place or person, just as a bank deposit will acquire interest if left in the bank for several years. This law of action and reaction is known popularly as the law of karma. The reactions in potential form are known as saṁskáras, or impressions in the mind.

Returning to the original question about life, death and possible rebirth, we are now in a better position to understand what happens at the time of death. According to the law of action and reaction we must experience the result of every action, and each day we are certainly experiencing pleasure and pain as the different impressions of the mind caused by previous actions become ripe and express themselves. If one were to die at a moment when all previous reactive momenta (saṁskáras) are exhausted and no new saṁskáras have been created, then the mind will be in a pure state and would merge in the Cosmic Consciousness. This state of permanent merger is known in Sanskrit as mokśa.

In reality, however, it is very difficult to exhaust all one's saṁskáras and not create new saṁskáras in the process. Whenever we perform an action with the feeling "I am doing this action," an impression is made on the mind. So in most cases when a person dies, he or she still has many reactions in potential form that have yet to be experienced. His or her mind is represented by the following diagram.

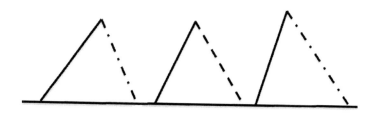

DIAGRAM 3

What will happen in such a case? The reactions must be experienced but there is no longer any physical body. So another body will be needed and the mind must take another birth.

In order to understand the process of rebirth it is necessary to understand life. According to Ánanda Márga philosophy, life is a parallelism between mind and body. There is a particular wavelength associated with the body, and there is a particular wavelength associated with the mind. Just as modern physics describes the world in terms of vibration, the yogis have said that this entire universe is vibrational and that the vibrations are of varying wavelengths. There is a particular wavelength associated with our body and there is a particular wavelength associated with our mind. When these wavelengths are parallel we have life. However, if something happens to the physical body, such as an accident or sickness, the physical wavelength may change and the parallelism may be lost. In this case we have what is known as the physical cause of death.

Physical wave

Mental wave

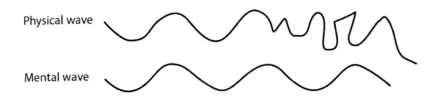

DIAGRAM 4: PHYSICAL CAUSE OF DEATH

Similarly the body may be functioning properly, but if there is a severe shock to the mind the mental wave may change and the parallelism is lost. This is known as the psychic cause of death. An example of this is a person dying due to having experienced something very fearful.

Physical wave

Mental wave

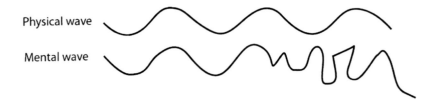

DIAGRAM 5: PSYCHIC CAUSE OF DEATH

Another example occurs when animals live with humans. A dog living with a human family is constantly in contact with the more developed human minds. The dog that lives, eats, and even travels with a human family begins to undergo an expansion of mind. His mind becomes gradually more and more human-like. If the expansion continues there may eventually be death due to a loss of parallelism between his mental and physical wavelengths. In this case the mental wavelength has changed due to contact with human beings and will consequently require a more subtle body with which it can find parallelism. This will probably be a human body.

There is another possibility, which is known as the spiritual cause of death. In highly evolved spiritual practitioners the mind will become absorbed in Cosmic Consciousness, which has a vibration of infinite wavelength represented as a straight line. If the mind attains prolonged parallelism with the Cosmic Entity, the person will lose parallelism with the physical body. In this case the person "leaves" his or her body and attains the state of mokśa. It is not a death in the sense of annihilation, but a merger into a state of infinite beatitude.

There is one more element that we must examine before we can fully understand the process of life, death and rebirth. Every living being not only has a physical body and a mind but also an *átman* or unit witnessing consciousness. This witnessing consciousness is the ultimate witness of the mind and is the source of the "I feeling" in the statement "I know that I exist." In an earlier chapter, the three functional parts of the mind have been discussed: citta (I have done), aham (I do) and mahat (I exist). The "I" that verifies the existence of these three functional parts of the mind is known as the átman. It is the imperishable unit consciousness and is the key to unlocking the mystery of life, death and rebirth.

When a person dies, the vital energy (prána) enters a state of disequilibrium and leaves the body. With the loss of the vital energy, the physical body ceases to function. The formerly living person loses all sense of pleasure, pain and self-consciousness. Although the mind enters a "long sleep" at the time of death, it has not perished as the physical body has. The samskáras—reactive momenta of the mind—still exist and are recorded in the causal mind. The átman remains as the witness of this inactive mind.

According to the type of samskáras, the inactive mind has a particular wavelength, and where there is a proper physical body anywhere in the universe that has a wavelength parallel to that of this mind, the mind will be reborn in this new body. The living being will then have the possibility to experience the potential reactions acquired in previous lifetimes.

How long will the interim period last? It can be very short or it can be thousands of years. The important thing is that there must be a suitable body somewhere in the cosmos that matches the vibration of the inactive disembodied mind and soul. In Tibetan Buddhism, as soon as a spiritual leader (lama) dies, his disciples search for his reincarnation in the form of a newly born baby. A suitable successor is groomed from among those young children who seem to have the same saṁskáras as the former lama. A test is given in which different objects, some of which belonged to the lama, are placed before the children. If the child can identify these objects, it is an indication that he may be the incarnation.

Another commonly asked question regarding reincarnation is whether one can remember his or her past lives. Up to the age of five years a person has *extra-cerebral memory*, which includes the memory of past lives. However, if this memory persists after the age of five, then a split personality would develop and the person would die. Thus, nature protects humans by not allowing this development of multiple personalities in a single body.

Although it may be fascinating to delve into our past lives, there is usually no particular psychological or spiritual value in doing so. Rather, it is generally advisable for spiritual aspirants to forget their past deeds (especially the bad ones) and to begin a life afresh, concentrating on the present and looking ahead to a more glorious future. Sometimes, however, in special cases a great spiritual master may "show" a disciple his or her past life in order to teach some lesson to him or her.

In his book *Ánanda Sútram,* Shrii Shrii Ánandamúrti describes the state of death as "the long sleep of the causal mind" and emphasizes that there is no feeling of pleasure and pain in this condition due to the loss of the organs and nerves. He also explains that these "bodiless" minds are without motor organs and that they cannot harm human beings.

As to heaven and hell, heaven is when we experience in this life the results of good actions of the past and hell is when we experience the results of past bad actions.

As is mentioned in the chapter on the cosmic cycle (Brahmacakra), the ultimate goal of this cycle of life and rebirth is the moment when the unit consciousness goes beyond life and rebirth and unifies with the unqualified Cosmic Consciousness.

Chapter 9

THE SIX SPOKES
OF SOCIETY

In the present era the pressing problems of humanity stem not only from lack of spiritual insight but also due to lack of proper understanding of social phenomena. Despite the long history of human existence dating back more than one million years, humanity has not yet been able to build a true society that can meet the multifarious needs of all its members.

In addition to his contribution in the field of spirituality, Shrii Shrii Ánandamúrti (writing under his civil name Prabhat Rainjan Sarkar) also addressed the important socioeconomic and cultural questions that trouble humanity today. He deftly identified the weaknesses that are leading humanity to apparent destruction. However, he was not a pessimist or a prophet of doom; rather he showed how spirituality, far from being a utopian ideal divorced from reality, can be the inspiration and guiding factor behind a new renaissance in all strata of human life.

Society *(samája* in Sanskrit) is defined by Ánandamúrti as the moving together of a group of people toward a cosmic goal. The spirit of society is like that of a group of pilgrims. If one of the pilgrims falls sick, the others will not leave him or her by the roadside but will make proper arrangements to care for that pilgrim, even if the whole group of pilgrims has to slow down. The larger society should have such a spirit so that not a single individual is allowed to lag behind. By this definition humanity has not yet built what we can call a "society."

Ánandamúrti observed that there are three needs for the construction of a true human society. The society must have a base for its existence *(asti),* a means for its development *(bhati)* and a goal toward which it is moving.

Lately, the very existence of civilization has been called into question. Some cosmologists say that perhaps there could be a thermal death of the universe in which the temperature would be the same in all parts of the universe. According to the Tantric concept of cosmology (as discussed in the chapter on Brahmacakra), this can never happen. This theory states that the manifest universe is a thought-wave emanating from the Cosmic Mind. Ánandamúrti emphasized that this macro-cosmic thought wave will go on for infinite time and that this thought wave cannot be retracted, i.e. the existence of the universe is assured. In addition, he pointed out that if a particular planet or dying star undergoes intense solidification, then this will result in *jadasphoía* (like a supernova) and new galaxies and stars will be created"There is no cause to fear," he said. "The earth may one day become extinct, but humanity cannot cease to exist." A particular solar system may die, but in that case it is likely that humanity will develop the means to move to other, more hospitable, solar systems.

Another more immediate threat to human civilization is atomic warfare. Here again Ánandamúrti is also hopeful for humanity's existence. He points out that atom bombs have been created by the human mind, which is much stronger than the bomb itself. He predicted that the same human mind that has created the atomic menace will in the near future also create devices to counteract the destructive power of nuclear weapons. However, he cautions that scientific research must be guided and controlled by moral people, not the warmongers who presently direct such activities.

Existence also implies that there will be proper arrangements for the basic necessities of life: food, shelter, clothing, education and medical care. Recent advances in human knowledge make it possible to guarantee the basic requirements of all people, yet social consciousness has lagged behind technological progress. For a large part of the world's population, even their existence is still in question. To deal with this problem, Ánandamúrti propounded a new economic philosophy known as the Progressive Utilization Theory (PROUT) (see chapter eleven).

For the development of society there are six factors or six spokes that make the wheel of society strong. When studying history we sometimes wonder why one civilization overcomes another, and why, for example, some invaders, such as the many groups that tried to attack the China, were sometimes absorbed by the civilization they were trying to conquer. The answer lies in the fact that some civilizations have been particularly strong in several of the six developmental factors and their collective psychology was able to overcome that of their rivals.

The first factor in developing society is spiritual ideology. Society needs a basic conception of the universe and of humanity's place in it. Humans must know what is their origin and also the goal toward which they are moving. Primitive societies had different creation myths and other societies evolved different religions and theologies to deal with these questions. To the extent that these philosophies can truly describe the meaning and purpose of human existence, that particular society will be able to develop successfully.

The second factor is spiritual practice. This is the complement of the first factor. It is not enough to tell humans that they can reach a certain state of being. One must also provide them with a practical means to realize their higher potential. Some societies have prayers and rituals that are practiced either by a few people or by the masses. The best situation would be to provide a rational, scientific practice that can be taught to many people. One great person does not make a great society. The elevation of as many people as possible through proper education and spiritual practice should be one of the fundaments of a sublime society.

The third factor is socio-economic theory. All societies must decide how scarce resources are to be allocated. Various theories, such as capitalism and Marxism, have evolved in the current era, but still the basic economic problems of humanity have not been properly dealt with. As mentioned earlier, Ánandamúrti offers PROUT, a spiritually based socio-economic system, as a replacement for the present systems that have not lived up to the hopes of their founders.

The fourth factor is social outlook. Without a proper social outlook even the best socio-economic ideas cannot be materialized. A healthy outlook is when one regards other living beings as his or her brothers and sisters. Such a fraternal feeling cannot be realized without spiritual practices, which provide inspiration and a means to liberate the mind from narrow feelings (see the following chapter on Neohumanism). Much of the chaos in present-day society is due to an improper social outlook.

The fifth factor is scripture. In Sanskrit, scripture is *shastra*, which literally means "that which liberates through discipline." All societies have codes of conduct presented in the teachings of their most enlightened members. These codes provide guidance and inspiration to all. To the extent that the codes are in conformity with cardinal human values and with basic human nature (dharma), then the society can develop in a healthy way. If in the name of scripture someone tries to impose codes of life that go against basic human values, then that society will head toward its destruction.

The last factor is preceptor, who is an embodiment of the values of the society. Preceptors are socio-spiritual leaders whose presence is vital to implementing the philosophy upon which society is based.

If any society is strong in these developmental factors then it can move toward the goal of divine bliss or ánandam. In this case, the society will endure for a longtime. Furthermore, those groups that have these six factors will be able to create spiritual leaders (sadvipras) who will be able to help humanity overcome any obstacle which may stand in its way.

Regarding the cosmic goal of ánandam (bliss), it is not possible that all of society will reach this goal at the same time. However, the cosmic goal should be in front of all and society must move in that direction. This cosmic ideal is the only ideal that can help unite humanity and keep it united for all time to come.

Chapter 10

NEOHUMANISM

One of the important factors in the development of any society is proper social outlook. In the past, entire civilizations have weakened and crumbled simply because one class or group considered another to be inferior and treated them as slaves. Today one of the greatest weaknesses of contemporary civilization is that there is no proper regard and mutual love among humans. Race is pitted against race, religion against religion, linguistic group against linguistic group. The divisions in human society are endless and they are sapping the vital life out of our civilization.

Not only is there a lack of mutual respect among people, but humans have lost all esteem, appreciation and responsibility toward the animals and plants who share this planet with us. Our wanton destruction of plant and animal life and our unthinking pollution of the air, earth, sea and space threaten to permanently damage the earth's ecosystem, making it inhospitable for all forms of life.

In his earliest writings on this subject, Ánandamúrti said that humans must think of themselves as part of one great family comprising all of humanity, rather than identifying with a particular race, religion, nationality or linguistic group. This type of social outlook he termed "universalism." In 1982 he further elaborated on the method of attaining universalism in a series of discourses published in the book *Liberation of Intellect: Neo-Humanism.* In that book he noted that traditional humanism has not been capable of elevating humanity to the height of universalism and presented a reformulated humanism based on spirituality, which he called neohumanism.

Neohumanism is a new formulation of traditional humanism. It is a spiritually based humanism with an ecological dimension. When human love is expanded to include not only all human beings but all other living beings, this is what Ánandamúrti calls neohumanism. Traditionally humanism meant cultivating respect for humanity. It arose as an alternative to religions that emphasized God in heaven but often neglected the plight of humans on earth. Proponents of humanism were often atheists or agnostics.

Neohumanism is derived from an understanding of the fundamental nature *(dharma)* of human beings. Human life has three aspects: physical, mental and spiritual. Regarding the physical aspect, the science of biology has already explained much about the workings of the human body. However, the psycho-spiritual needs of humans have not been fully understood up until now, despite the efforts of psychologists and spiritual seekers.

The higher possibilities of human nature demand that the mind be free to expand and to flow toward the Supreme Consciousness (God). When this happens, a human being develops love (devotion) for the Supreme Consciousness and love for all other beings. This love for the Supreme Consciousness should be considered to be the most valuable treasure of humanity. Without it life becomes dry and meaningless.

Today, however, humanity does not have a proper philosophy of life, and so our society is not in harmony with the inner longings of the human heart. Materialism pervades all parts of present-day life and materialism is crushing the devotional sentiment in humans. As a result of this imbalance between the inner needs and outer realities, we find much misery, depression and mental illness in society.

The solution to rectifying this imbalance is a philosophy that harmonizes the inner needs of humanity with the outer demands of the material world. In order to implement such a way of life, we must know the ways in which the spiritual treasure (devotion) of humanity is threatened. Neohumanism is the philosophy of life that unites inner spirituality with the demands of the outer environment. It is the philosophy of life that will enable people to develop themselves fully and at the same time become true universalists, seeing themselves as part of a vast cosmic family. There are, however, three human sentiments that impede the expansion of the human mind toward this universalistic, neohumanistic outlook.

When one is obsessed with one's geographical land, this is called *geosentiment*. In the past, and even today, many people were concerned only with their own land or own country. Out of this love of their land they evolved other subsentiments, such as geopatriotism, geopolitics, georeligion and geoeconomics. Using geo-patriotism to stir the masses, politicians have goaded them into fighting many bloody wars. The colonialism of the past and the neocolonialism of today is nothing but a form of geoeconomics. "Let us develop our own country even if it creates misery and poverty in satellite states" is the slogan behind geoeconomics.

Another sentiment that has harmed humanity is called *sociosentiment*. Here people focus their attention on the particular social group to which they belong. It may be a national, linguistic, social or religious group. Although this sentiment is sometimes more expansive than geosentiment (if the particular social group happens to be very large), it still creates a group consciousness that comes into conflict with the sentiment of other groups. The religious wars of the past and even of the present were and are caused by this sociosentiment.

Finally, the expansion of the human mind is blocked by another seemingly "good" sentiment, that is, "humanism." Love and respect for other human beings, or "humanism," should be a noble sentiment uniting humanity and elevating the minds of everyone. However, ordinary humanism has some serious shortcomings.

First of all, such humanism does not extend to plants and animals. People talk of "human rights" but continue to deny the rights of plants and animals to exist.

In the book *Liberation of Intellect*, Ánandamúrti observes that humans are eager to preserve the lives of animals that have utility value to them. A cow that gives milk is useful, but if that cow ceases to give milk, then she will be slaughtered because that cow has no more "utility value" to humans. However, all creatures want to live and preserve their lives, just as we do. These creatures have existential value; their own existence gives them value, whether they are our friends or enemies. According to neohumanism, we should recognize this value and not wantonly destroy living creatures that are not directly useful to us. Due to the foolishness of the present economic system, humanity is clearing the forests for short-term gains, not realizing that our own existence may be threatened by such actions.

This recognition of the existential value of all living beings gives neohumanism its ecological dimension and is an important addition to previous understandings of what it means to be a humanist.

Another defect of ordinary humanism is that, bereft of a strong spiritual background, it often degenerates into pseudohumanism. For example, many so-called developed nations give foreign aid to less developed countries in the name of humanism, but behind the scenes the multinational corporations of these same nations are extracting all the wealth out of the less developed nations, creating extensive misery for people and massive ecological destruction in their reckless pursuit of profits.

Nations go to war, killing millions of people, under the banners of peace and democracy! This kind of hypocrisy is an extreme example of pseudo-humanism. It is important to penetrate behind the words and understand what is really happening.

Ánandamúrti has done more than describe the problems caused by these limited sentiments. He also presents ways to overcome the sentiments that stand in the way of our developing universalistic consciousness. He says that geosentiments can only be countered

when humans develop their faculty of rationality. Rational thinking
is an extremely valuable tool that humans have at their disposal.
Through proper study and use of the mind, humans can easily see
through the geosentiments propagated by demagogues.

In this regard, Ánandamúrti emphasizes that mental analysis
must not be checked by dogmas, which he defines as ideas or
belief systems that attempt to limit the field of human thinking.
In some countries, for example, one may discuss economics only
within the framework of a certain philosophy. This is a dogma, not
very different from the religious dogmas of some countries where
spiritual or social ideas can only be discussed within the bounds
laid out by a particular religious faith. All dogmas, whether they
are presented as religious or even claimed to be "scientific" are
dangerous for human welfare.

Regarding social sentiments, the best way to overcome them
is by adhering to the principle of social equality (*sama-samája
tattva*). Amongst humans, two principal psychologies can be
observed. Some people live only for their own selfish pleasure
and never think of the needs or rights of others. A loftier outlook
is where people have a determination to move toward the Supreme
Consciousness, and along the way they make a resolve to elim-
inate the social inequalities that divide humanity. Ánandamúrti
explains that the "endeavor to advance toward the ultimate reality
by forming a society free from all inequalities with all members of
the human race moving in unison is called *Sama Samaj Tattva.*"[18]

Thus, socio-sentiments can only be overcome with the spiritual
outlook inherent in sama-samája tattva. The key to removing
social inequalities is a "proto-spiritual mentality." Proto-spiritual
mentality is the attempt to focus the mind on a spiritual object
(the Supreme Consciousness). When this kind of thought becomes
the reality of human life, then sociosentiments can be easily
surmounted.

In order to overcome the defects of ordinary humanistic sentiments, humans will have to first accept that all creatures have
existential value. That is, all creatures have a right to live in the

18   P. R. Sarkar, *Liberation of Intellect: Neo-Humanism* (Calcutta: Ananda
Marga Publications, 1982).

world and develop according to their inherent nature. Humans will have to take steps to see that the habitats of animals and plants are not destroyed, even if these plants and animals have no apparent utility value to humans.

To fight against pseudo-humanism, we will have to be motivated by spirituality (movement of the mind toward the Supreme Consciousness). Humanism cannot remain an intellectual concept; rather it must be nourished by a flow of love. When one does spiritual practices, love for all beings arises within, and when this is expressed in individual and collective life, then spirituality becomes humanity's mission and universalism is attained.

Ánandamúrti presented neohumanism as the solution to the world›s social problems and described the ways in which many social, political and religious leaders have been trying to block the progress of humanity through dogmas, pseudo-humanism, pseudo-spirituality and halfhearted and incomplete reform measures. Despite the dismal record of present and past leaders we should remain optimistic, because once humanity accepts the Cosmic Consciousness as the goal of life and collectively moves toward that goal, we will overcome all obstacles, small and large.

Chapter 11

PROUT: A NEW SOCIOECONOMIC THEORY

One of the necessary factors in the development of a healthy society is a proper socio-economic theory. In any age, people have to come to grips with the question of how the resources of the world are to be utilized and allocated. In addition, society needs a system of government that can meet the needs of all its members. The answers society gives to these concerns reflects the socioeconomic values that society follows.

During the twentieth century, proponents of two economic theories competed for dominance. Capitalism, which had already been around for more than two hundred years, was challenged by Marxism. The world was almost incinerated in a nuclear disaster due to this rivalry, and when the Cold War came to an end in 1990 many people breathed a sigh of relief. But, the demise of Marxism didn't mean that a golden age had arrived for humanity. The Marxist challenge to capitalism had come about due to serious flaws in an economic system that concentrated wealth into the hands of a small minority of people while millions lived in poverty and misery. The collapse of Marxism did nothing to alleviate the defects of capitalism.

During the era of the Cold War, some emerging nations formed the Nonaligned Movement and stated their wish to remain independent from the competing Marxist and capitalists powers. That movement foundered because they could not come up with an alternative to capitalism or Marxism. At the same moment when the Non-Aligned Movement was created, Shrii Shrii Ánandamúrti, writing under his civil name, P.R. Sarkar, gave a series of lectures later published in the book *Idea and Ideology* in which he described a socio-economic theory that he called the Progressive Utilization Theory, known by the acronym PROUT.

Although it may seem that PROUT has similarities with existing socio-economic philosophies, a deep understanding of Sarkar's ideas shows that PROUT stands alone in the world today, in that it is based on a spiritual rather than materialistic conception of the universe and of humanity. The idea that all animate and inanimate objects are part of one Supreme Consciousness and are to be treated as part of an integrated whole is the base of PROUT. Just as capitalism and Marxism emerged in an era when physicists and philosophers held a materialistic and mechanistic outlook, PROUT is emerging at a time when humanity is beginning to accept a holistic and spiritual view of the universe. This holistic and spiritual base helps to define a new view of economics, history and political leadership and offers the hope that humanity can find a way out of the present socio-economic crisis.

One way to understand PROUT is to consider Sarkar's definitions of the words *progress, utilization* and *theory*. According to Sarkar, progress, in its true sense, takes place on the spiritual plane because it is only there that one can move toward a goal without provoking a counter-movement. In the physical sphere, on the other hand, there is development, such as the invention of the automobile, but this development is always accompanied by negative repercussions, such as car pollution and the increased risk of injury and death in accidents.

In the mental or psychic sphere there is also development, such as the increase of knowledge among the masses in the contemporary era, but once again there are negative results of this development, such as the increase in stress, psychic complexes and mental illness that accompanies mental development. The idea of progress, as defined by Sarkar, is for humans to adjust to changing developments in the physical and psychic worlds while moving toward a spiritual goal.

Utilization means that the resources of the universe should be used to promote the good and happiness of all, not just a few. And utilization of resources also applies to supramundane, spiritual and psychic potentialities, which are commonly neglected in many economic approaches.

Some theories are good in the theoretical realm but cannot be materialized in the practical world due to changing circumstances. A theory that was developed after observing the economic situation of the nineteenth century may no longer apply in the twenty-first century. Some theories have been advanced by hypocrites who never had any intention to materialize their theory, while others were put forward by logicians who were content to live in an abstract world and thus these theories have no practical utility for society.

Sarkar contends that the best kind of theory is one that is based on a careful assessment of events in the world and which also has a built-in capacity to adjust to changing environmental circumstances. The Progressive Utilization Theory is such a theory. It is based on observation of society and also has within it the means to maintain adjustment with changes in the world.

PROUT incorporates these concepts of progress and of utilization in a theory that is defined in five fundamental principles:

1. *No individual should be allowed to accumulate any physical wealth without the clear permission or approval of the collective body.*

This principle strikes at the fundamental weakness of capitalism, which allows a few individuals to accumulate wealth even if it results in the starvation of millions. It clearly establishes the basis of a collective approach to economic questions. While the principle calls for limitations on the individual possession of physical wealth, which is something finite, it does not call for limitations on wealth in the mental and spiritual sphere, because these are infinite treasures of humanity that should not be restricted. In Marxism this distinction between physical and psychic wealth was not understood, and the severe restrictions placed on freedom of thought and religion led to the downfall of most systems based on this theory.

2. *There should be maximum utilization and rational distribution of all mundane, supramundane and spiritual potentialities of the universe.*

This principle encourages society to utilize all resources of the universe to satisfy human needs. Rational distribution means that the minimum necessities should be guaranteed to all but that individuals who have contributed special services to society should be given special rewards to encourage their work and to encourage others also to contribute more to society. Rational distribution does not mean equal distribution.

3. *There should be maximum utilization and rational distribution of all physical, metaphysical and spiritual potentialities of the unit and collective bodies of human society.*

This principle refers to the utilization of human resources and states that a healthy society must develop the potentialities of all people. By denying large segments of humanity the chance for educational and economic development, the present-day society is not correctly utilizing precious human resources. This principle also calls attention to the need to balance collective good with individual good.

4. *There should be a proper adjustment amongst these physical, metaphysical, mundane, supramundane, and spiritual utilizations.*

Here Sarkar is saying that society should inspire people to work for the individual and collective good, and thus he urges that provisions be made so that all can earn their minimum necessities through appropriate work. This principle also calls for society to make proper use of comparatively rare faculties such as spirituality.

5. *The method of utilization should vary in accordance with changes in time, space and person, and the utilization should be of a progressive nature.*

This principle provides society with a means of adapting to changing circumstances and also calls on humans to utilize scientific research guided by neohumanism in order to bring about the welfare of all.

Economy of PROUT

How the principles of PROUT can be applied in society is for the moment a theoretical question, as no country as yet has embraced PROUT. Also, the means of implementing PROUT will vary from age to age. However, in Sarkar's writings and in the writings of other Proutist commentators we can see how the principles of PROUT could be used to bring about an economic system that can best be described as Progressive Socialism: a non-Marxist socialism based on neohumanism.

In his writings on industrial and economic policy, Sarkar has stressed the need to prevent economic exploitation. He says that the important economic enterprises that supply people with their basic necessities of life should not be placed in the hands of private enterprise. Sarkar was also aware of the failings of central governments to directly control such enterprises.

To organize an economy on Proutist lines requires a three-tiered economy. Small enterprises employing few people and which do not deal with essential goods and services can be managed and owned as private businesses (e.g., a small restaurant).

The second tier, which consists of the majority of enterprises, would be set up as cooperatives, owned and managed by the people who work in the industries. The workers would be the stockholders of these businesses and would choose the management just as stockholders do today. The third category consists of the largest enterprises that employ large amounts of people and have important effects on various parts of the economy — key industries, such as steel production, energy, transport, etc. These should be managed by either autonomous public boards or by local governments, but not by central governments. This category would run on a no-profit, no-loss basis.

Such a system would also follow the principle of economic decentralization and this could be accomplished by reorganizing the economy on the basis of self-sufficient economic zones in which there would be balanced agricultural, industrial, and service sectors.

The idea of the Proutist economy is to provide a good standard of living to all people and to see that economic power is not concentrated in the hands of a few.

Theory of History and Government

To bring such a system into being requires new governmental arrangements. Various socialistic experiments of the nineteenth and twentieth centuries ended up in failure, disappointment and worse. How this can be avoided in the future is best understood by examining P. R. Sarkar's new interpretation of history, which he delineates in the book *Human Society.*

Sarkar said that history can be understood as the cyclical dominance of the different classes of society. His concept of class is, however, far different from previous, materialistic ideas of class. Sarkar defines class by mental characteristics rather than physical or materialistic concerns. He says that at the dawn of humanity the dominant mentality or class was that of the *shudras*—people in whom matter is dominant over mind. These people were primarily concerned with the struggle to survive. Throughout history the toiling people concerned with physical survival belong to this class of shudras or workers.

Sarkar noted that leadership of society then passed into the hands of people with another mentality. The class of *kṣattriyas* (warriors) developed the mentality that "with my physical force I will overcome the world (matter)." From the time of the Neolithic period and throughout the ancient world this class ruled society. The chronicles of wars fought by the great civilizations of the Middle East are an example of this age of warriors.

With the further evolution of society another class became predominant. The *vipras* or intellectuals had a different approach to the conquest. They thought, "With my mental force I will overcome the world." In the Middle Ages, ministers, advisors or priests (popes, imams, etc.) held the real power even though warrior-kings were often the nominal rulers. This intellectual class brought new psychic and sometimes spiritual ideas, but they also exploited society and were responsible for the religious wars of that time.

The cycle of society is always moving. The intellectuals ceded their authority to a class of *vaeshyas* or capitalists who created the industrial and commercial revolutions that ushered in the modern age. The mentality of this class is to use mental strength to accumulate wealth. Just as the warrior age had a particular type of government—monarchy—and the intellectual age had its variation of monarchy which Sarkar calls *ministocracy,* the age of capitalism saw the rise of democracy. Currently almost all countries of the world are in the capitalist era.

According to Sarkar, this vaeshyan era is near its end, and it will finish with social revolution led by the economically, politically and psychologically oppressed masses. Following this revolution, the age of warriors will come again.

But is the future of civilization so dim that we can only expect continuous revolution and military dictatorship in the future? Sarkar's theory holds forth another possibility. He said that the best arrangement is for the evolution of a declassed human whom he called the *sadvipra*. The sadvipra is a spiritually and morally based revolutionary who works against the exploitation of any particular class. The problem with most social changes in the past is that inevitably the class that initiated the change eventually ended up exploiting the other segments of society. The only way to avoid this is to create sadvipras who will work for the rights of all.

The political concept of PROUT is based on establishing an electorate composed of spiritually developed people. The democracy of the present day will undergo reform. Democracy, although better than any other system yet introduced, has a number of weaknesses. First of all, there is no provision for the economic rights of the people and democracy has even been the preferred government of powerful economic interests who can easily buy their way into influence and power. In addition, there are three basic qualities often lacking in the electorate that ensures that a poor standard of leaders is elected year after year.

The three qualities are as follows:

- *Education:* where many illiterate or uneducated people vote, unscrupulous politicians take advantage and get votes easily through dishonest practices. This is particularly prevalent in the less economically developed countries.
- *Morality* is another quality that is missing. If more than 51 percent of people are dishonest, then dishonest people can be elected.
- Another missing ingredient is *socio-economic-political consciousness.* Mere education is not enough. Those voting must know what they are voting for, or else they will easily be misled by opportunistic politicians. Thus Sarkar says that the standard of education, morality and socio-economic consciousness must be raised and from among such a public, real leaders with the spirit of social service (the sadvipra) can then emerge and serve society. With such universalistic leadership, humanity can reverse the weaknesses of the present period and will be able to set up a social and economic system that is rational, just and truly progressive.

In a nutshell, I have described the socio-economic theory that Shrii Shrii Ánandamúrti put forward as the solution to present-day problems. Will it actually come about and will humanity build a society in which all people get a chance to live in peace and security and develop themselves fully? I can't predict the future but I agree with my teacher who was an incorrigible optimist and declared, "Let the blackness of the new-moon night be lifted from the path of the downtrodden. Let the new human beings of a new day wake up to a new sunrise in a new world."[19]

19   P. R. Sarkar, *Human Society, Part 2* (Calcutta: Ananda Marga Publications, 1967).

Acknowledgments

Thanks to all friends and colleagues who helped me in the production of *The Wisdom of Tantra*. The present volume is largely based on the 1990 version, which was entitled *The Wisdom of Yoga*, and I thank Dada Jyotirupananda and Dada Maheshvarananda for their assistance in publishing that forerunner to the present edition. I also deeply appreciate the help of Andy Douglas, Dada Gunamuktananda, and Taraka Ghista, all of whom spent time proofreading the present manuscript and making suggestions for its improvement. Many thanks go to Aaron (Ananta) Staengl for drawing the illustrations, diagrams, and the cover image. I am once again grateful to Donald Devashish Acosta for his expert editing, layout work, and handling of the details of publishing the finished book. My greatest debt, though, is to my guru, Shrii Shrii Anandamurti, because all that I have written in these pages is based on his ideas and concepts—it would have taken me many lifetimes to learn these things unaided.

Glossary

Ágama: the practical books of Tantra; the replies of Shiva to the questions of Párvatii in Tantra scriptures.

Ahaṁ, ahaṁtattva: doer "I", ego, second mental subjectivity, the "I do" portion of the Cosmic Mind or unit mind.

Ahiṁsá: not to inflict harm on others; the first principle of Yama.

Aparigraha: nonaccumulation of wealth that is superfluous to our actual needs.

Ásana: yoga posture; literally "a position in which one feels easy."

Aśtáuṇga yoga: eight-limbed yoga.

Asteya: non-stealing.

Atimánasa kośa: the first layer of the superconscious mind.

Bhágavata Dharma: the innate tendency that leads human beings towards the Supreme Entity.

Brahma Tadsthiti: realization of the Supreme.

Cakra (Chakra): cycle or circle; psycho-spiritual center, or plexus.

Citta, cittatattva: the mental plate; the "I have done" portion of the Cosmic Mind or unit mind.

Dháraṅá: concentration on a point; Dháraṅá literally means "locating the mind firmly in an area or region of the body."

Dharma: innate characteristic, nature of a thing. The dharma of fire is to burn; the spiritual dharma of human beings is to realize the Supreme Consciousness.

Dhyána: meditation in which the psyche is directed toward Consciousness; seventh limb of eight-limbed yoga.

Devayoni: luminous bodies; literally "an entity with divine qualities."

Diikśá: spiritual initiation; "The process which produces the capacity to realize the inner import of mantra and which expedites the requital of the saḿskáras, or reactive momenta, is called diikśá."

Diipajiṋánam: the light of knowledge.

Guru: the one who dispels darkness, a spiritual teacher.

Hiraṅmaya kośa: the third layer of the superconscious mind.

Idá: The left nádii (psychic nerve or channel) running up the body and crisscrossing the spine.

Iishvara praṅidhána: to make the Cosmic Consciousness the goal of your life; meditation on the Supreme Consciousness.

Jaḋasphoťa: explosion of matter; a reaction within a physical body resulting in structural dissociation.

Kámamaya kośa: conscious mind.

Kárána mánas: causal mind; super-conscious mind.

Kuṅḋalinii, kulakuṅḋalinii: the sleeping divine energy of an individual living being. Literally, "coiled serpentine"; sleeping divinity; the force dormant in the base of the body, which, when awakened, rises up the spinal column to develop all one's spiritual potentialities.

Lalita Mármika: the dance performed while singing kiirtan.

Madya: one of the 5 Ms; literally "wine" or divine nectar.

Maethuna: one of the 5 Ms; In subtle Tantra, the union of individual consciousness and cosmic consciousness; sexual union.

Máḿsa: one of the 5 Ms; meat.

Mánava: human, as in mánava dharma (human dharma)

Manomaya kośa: subconscious mind.

Mantra: a sound vibration that liberates the mind.

Mantrágháta: the striking power of the mantra.

Mantra caetanya: to imbibe the proper spirit of a mantra; to understand the meaning of the mantra.

Matsya: one of the 5 Ms; fish or in subtle Tantra, pranayama (breath control).

Mahákaola: a guru who has elevated his or her kundalini and who can elevate the kundalini of any other person.

Mokśa: salvation, permanent liberation, non-qualified liberation.

Mudrá: one of the 5 Ms; keeping company with spiritual people (satsauṇga); gesture in Indian dance; a yogic exercise; "Shunning of bad company is called mudrá sádhaná."

Nigama: the theoretical books of Tantra; in Tantric scripture, the questions posed by Párvatii to Lord Shiva.

Nirguńa Brahma: Brahma unaffected by the guńas; non-qualified Brahma.

Nirvikalpa samádhi: absorption of the unit mind into the witnessing consciousness (átman).

Piuṇgalá: The right nádii (psychic nerve or channel) running up the body and crisscrossing the spine.

Oṇṁkára: the primordial sound (Om); the sound of the first vibration of creation; the seed mantra of the expressed universe; **Oṇṁkára** literally means "the sound oṇm."

Prakrti: cosmic operative principle.

Práńáh: the collective name of the vital energies in a living body.

Práńáyáma: yogic breath control; control of vital energy; "The process by which the práńás in the body are controlled is called práńáyáma."

Pratyáhára: withdrawing the mind from attachment to external objects.

Práńendriya: the collectivity of the vital energy in the human body that is centered in the anáhata cakra.

Pratisaiṇcara: movement towards the cosmic nucleus.

Prout: the progressive utilization theory.

Puruśottama: the nucleus of the universe; Nucleus Consciousness.

Rasa: flow.

Rishi (rśi): a sage, one who, by inventing new things, broadens the path of progress of human society.

Sádhaná: literally, "sustained effort"; spiritual practice; meditation.

Saguńa Brahma: Brahma with qualities; Brahma affected by the guńas.

Saiṇcara: movement away from the cosmic nucleus; in the Cosmic Cycle, the step-by-step extroversion and crudification of consciousness from the Nucleus Consciousness to the state of solid matter (saiṇcara literally means "movement").

Sama-samája tattva: the principle of social equality.

Samája: society.

Samádhi: absorption of the unit mind into the Cosmic Mind (savikalpa samádhi) or into the átman (nirvikalpa samádhi). There are also various kinds of samádhis that involve only partial absorption and have their own distinguishing characteristics, according to the technique or spiritual practice followed.

Saṁskára: mental reactive momentum, potential mental reaction.

Satya: action of mind and the use of speech in the spirit of welfare; benevolent truthfulness.

Santośa: to maintain a state of mental ease; contentment of mind.

Sattvaguńa: the sentient principle.

Savikalpa samádhi: the state of partial absorption of mind; absorption of the unit mind into the Cosmic Mind.

Sevá: service.

Shaoca: cleanliness of body and purity of mind.

Shástra: scriptures; that which liberates through discipline.

Suśumná: the central nerve that runs up the spine and extends up to the crown of the head; the psycho-spiritual channel within the spinal column through which the kulakuńdalinii rises during meditation.

Svádhiśthána cakra: the second, or fluida, psycho-spiritual center or plexus.

Svádhyáya: clear understanding of a spiritual subject; spiritual self-study.

Tańdava: a jumping dance for men first taught by Shiva.

Táraka Brahma: the Supreme Entity in its liberating aspect.

Tantra: the spiritual practice that liberates people through the expansion of mind; a spiritual tradition that originated in India in prehistoric times and was first systematized by Shiva. It emphasizes the development of human vigor, both through meditation and through confrontation of difficult external situations, to overcome all fears and weaknesses; also, a scripture expounding that tradition.

Tattva: one of the five basic factors (solid, liquid, luminous, aerial, ethereal).

Tattva dháraná: a yogic process of concentration on the controlling points of the five factors in the human body.

Tejas tattva: luminous factor.

Vaerágya: the practice whereby we develop detachment from finite objects.

Váyu: wind; vital airs in the human body.

Vayu tattva: the gaseous factor.

Veda: Literally, "knowledge"; hence, a composition imparting spiritual knowledge. Also, a religious or philosophical school that originated among the Aryans and was brought by them to India. It is based on the Vedas and emphasizes the use of ritual to gain the intervention of the gods.

Vijiṇánamaya kośa: the second layer of the superconscious mind.

Viveka: discernment, conscience.

Vrtti: mental propensity.

Vistára: expansion of mind.

Yama: "that which controls." The first five principle of moral conduct in yoga.

CPSIA information can be obtained
at www.ICGtesting.com
Printed in the USA
FFOW02n2156110516
24000FF